The Diamonds Within Us

The Diamonds Within Us sparkles with personal experience, accessible practices, and an approach to psychology grounded in brilliant, unconditional health. In sharing her own lifelong journey through the inception and development of Contemplative Psychology, Melissa Moore also passes on the radical experiments incubated at Naropa University and expressed in Karuna Training, experiments now matured and weathered through decades of learning. Both rooted in a strong lineage and sensitive to the demands of our present, this book also gestures toward Contemplative Psychology's future as we face ecological loss, unconscious bias, and cultural fragmentation.

—**ADAM LOBEL, PhD**

The Diamonds Within Us is a rich treasure trove of the exquisite depth of understanding of an embodied meditation practitioner and teacher of the [Buddhist] Contemplative Psychology tradition. Dr. Moore's thorough step-by-step elucidations on the skandhas, emptiness, the Buddha Families, and transmutation are a complete transmission of Buddhist psychology and engages readers to mine their own exquisite goodness in the midst of personal and societal confusion. By making friends with ourselves, as Dr. Moore advocates, we see that sparkling neurosis is our diamond in the rough!

—**JANNELI CHAPIN,** Assistant Professor, Contemplative Psychotherapy and Buddhist Psychology Program, Naropa University

Dr. Moore's excellent book, *The Diamonds Within Us*, is a crystallization of her many years of work as the creator and primary facilitator of Karuna Training, a program that instructs us how to befriend and love ourselves and practice engaged compassion with others. This book guides us step-by-step in the practice of meditation, revealing how we can embrace the experience of nowness, the timeless moment where we have immediate access to the truth of our experience. The good news is that by following the instructions in this book, we can discover that our minds are workable and that our emotions can provide an operating system to navigate our lives. Dr. Moore's book offers explanations for how to cultivate authenticity in ourselves and how to be of service to others at a time when the world desperately needs compassion.

—IRA RECHTSHAFFER, PHD, author of *Mindfulness and Madness: Money, Food, Sex, and the Sacred*

In *The Diamonds Within Us*, Dr. Moore gives us a compelling and highly readable exposition of the inner workings of Contemplative Psychology. Drawing on her many years working in challenging clinical settings, devising curricula, and teaching Karuna Training throughout Europe and North America, she develops here a rigorous yet highly compassionate and dignified alternative to more diagnostically driven narratives around psychological suffering.

—JAMES O'NEIL, author of *Undressing*

When so many of us are confronted daily by a deluge of divisive politics and strong emotions, the message of compassion in this book couldn't be more on point. Dr. Melissa Moore offers an empowering view of the mind and healing beyond pathology. Drawn from the wealth of the Buddhist Mahayana and Vajrayana tradition, *The Diamonds Within Us* is a treatise on the meaning of intrinsic health skillfully rendered for anyone seeking a direct path for working with pain.

—SILAS ROSE, *Awake in Relationship* Podcast

Melissa Moore's *The Diamonds Within Us* is a brilliant, colorful exploration of Contemplative Psychology and Karuna Training, two approaches close to my own heart. Through powerful, personal honesty, along with examples and lessons from 40 years of learning and teaching, Moore's book delivers the pickaxe and polishing cloths we need to begin to dig out and shine our own jewels.

—MIRIAM HALL, co-author of *Heart of Photography*

The Diamonds Within Us

Uncovering Brilliant Sanity
Through Contemplative Psychology

Melissa Moore, PhD

Edited by Emily Earlenbaugh, PhD

modern wisdom
PRESS

Modern Wisdom Press
Boulder, Colorado, USA
www.modernwisdompress.com

Published 2021
Cover Design: Karen Polaski, KP Design
Author's photo courtesy of Benjamin D. Buren - AliveStudios.Com

DISCLAIMER
Neither the author nor the publisher assumes any responsibility for errors, omissions, or contrary interpretations of the subject matter within.

MEDICAL DISCLAIMER
The information in this book is a result of years of practical experience by the author. This information is not intended as a substitute for the advice provided by your physician or other healthcare professional. Do not use the information in this book for diagnosing or treating a health problem or disease, or prescribing medication or other treatment.

I dedicate this book to my Buddhist teachers.

Chögyam Trungpa Rinpoche,
Tsultrim Gyatso Rinpoche,
who brought me the dharma,

Also, to Dr. Ed Podvoll,
who dared to live the teachings,

and to "space"
for the basic sanity
you've provided me on the path.

Table of Contents

Foreword

I met Melissa Moore 40 years ago on the first day of our Master's Program in Contemplative (Buddhist and Western) Psychology. We had no idea at the time how life-transforming that journey would be, but we shared a reckless yearning to find out how to be sane, authentically sane, not the kind that's packaged as "normal." We had landed in the right place at the right time. For the next two and a half years, we were guided by Dr. Ed Podvoll, who was uncompromisingly dedicated to a path of discovering intrinsic health within our confusion rather than holding out the carrot of self-improvement. This sounds like a radical approach, but it is rooted in Buddhist psychology, with research going back thousands of years provided by meditators who were willing to sit and look directly at their own minds.

As Melissa and I found out, this unmasking process can sometimes be painful, but learning to ride the ups and downs of our everyday experience became more workable as the weeks and months rolled by. We emerged from our training with a glimmer of confidence not only that this path could restore our own sanity but also that we could find ways to offer it to others. Just before our graduation, Ed commented that we hadn't learned any of the techniques usually taught in graduate school. Instead, we had learned the essence of what it means to be present and to trust the space and heart of relationship.

After graduation, Melissa and I headed off in separate directions: I moved to Alaska, and she relocated to Europe. We met each other again 25 years later. Then I discovered how she had grown these teachings on Buddhist psychology forward in a program called Karuna Training. Melissa brought her characteristic blend of playfulness, self-honesty, and steadiness along to the task of building these communities. I gratefully accepted when she invited me to join her teaching staff. It was heartening to see how the participants were engaging with the same instructions Melissa and I received from Ed so many years earlier and how beautifully those seeds were blossoming. I appreciated that these trainings in compassion were not framed as therapy. Though many professionals are attracted to them, they're open to anyone who wants a community of support for personal development. As a teacher, I've witnessed how successful this training has been for hundreds of people.

Now, at last, Melissa has masterfully brought her teachings and the depth of her personal experience into this book. It's important to reflect on how challenging it is to produce a book of this kind. The topic of Contemplative Psychology isn't another variation on what most of us associate with conventional psychotherapy. Nor is it an offshoot of the popular mindfulness movement. Even students of Buddhism who are familiar with some of the core teachings will discover a fresh opportunity to look more closely at how their own minds and hearts function in relationship. This is the key point: Contemplative Psychology is about the essence of human relationships, the experience of coming home to who we really are in the context of our connection to each other. It presents the view that we human beings are intrinsically sane rather than fundamentally broken. This is radically different from our conventional assumptions. The task of discovering our true nature requires commitment and support, but what is most important is to have a clear understanding of what this journey looks like.

The Diamonds Within Us accomplishes this. This book is not only a brilliant, comprehensive description of a path of personal transformation, but it is also infused with innovative language and personal stories that come from the heart of direct experience. Reading it, I can hear Melissa's voice, feel her humor and her kindness. I'm grateful for her decades of hard work and compassion in bringing these instructions on the path of Contemplative Psychology forward in such a complete way. The world needs these teachings now more than ever.

—Susan Gillis Chapman
author of *The Five Keys to Mindful Communication*

Introduction

I was 25 years old when I entered the master's degree program at Naropa Institute (now Naropa University) in Boulder, Colorado. At the time, I didn't aspire to be a therapist; I only wanted to be part of a burgeoning scene in Boulder connected to Naropa Institute. The scene was being stirred up by a magic man, a Tibetan Rinpoche[1] named Chögyam Trungpa. Rinpoche founded Naropa Institute with a pedagogy that combined insight with intuition through the practice of meditation, and it was primarily an alternative art institute offering study in Buddhism, Buddhist meditation, poetry, dance, theater, and Buddhist psychology. As I've often said, teams of horses couldn't have kept me away.

Learning to embrace intensity in every moment and embrace the potency of transitions is the journey of Contemplative Psychology. As a young student at Naropa, I remember one of the instructors, Judy Leif, saying, "The entire reason we practice meditation is to prepare for our death." She was teaching on the Tibetan Bardo experience of transitions between death and rebirth. At 25, death was the last thing I wanted to think about! However, in Contemplative Psychology, we understand our impermanent, permeable, groundless nature is our saving grace. We learn to navigate the unpredictable transitions of life as a creative dance, and through life, now at 64, I notice that life's transitions are ceaseless.

In retrospect, I now see the culture around Chögyam Trungpa was reckless and harmful to many. Yet, I still find value and depth in these indestructible teachings, which are pure beyond human indiscretion. Many people seek greater meaning, deeper connection with

---

1 Rinpoche—an honorific in Tibetan Buddhism for an incarnate teacher or lama.

others, and less self-consciousness in everyday life. I bear witness in my trainings to a slice of society in the first half of the 21st century that is making a significant transition of awareness that necessitates a change in human consciousness. Between climate change, natural disasters, catastrophic political extremes, systemic racism, and surviving a worldwide pandemic, it's easy to find oneself feeling powerless and lost. We genuinely ponder, "How can I help, either myself or those in need in the world? How can I contribute without driving myself entirely to the brink of insanity?"

We can feel overwhelmed in the face of change and the recognition that changes do not affect everyone equally. However, the ability to tolerate a rapidly changing environment with agility and ease is of substantial benefit to oneself, and helpful to others. Developing flexibility and the ability to meet intensity are reasons to practice Contemplative Psychology.

We might think that learning about something as self-reflective and spacious as meditation is a waste of time in the face of the world's problems. But Contemplative Psychology offers ways of seeing and being that aid us in engaging with the profound struggles of our era. Contemplative Psychology is a path of transforming our emotions into their innate wisdom. It supports humanity by offering heart-opening methods that meet everyday social dilemmas. In Compassionate Exchange, the central practice of Contemplative Psychology, we truly support one another in meeting our individual and collective challenges.

Today, we as human beings (really, as all species) are being pressure-cooked on global and societal levels. At a time when we can connect to people around the world in a moment, I also see we're starving to death, as a species, for genuine heart connection with others. We all can give and receive a natural love, and Contemplative Psychology is a path dedicated to uncovering this innate potential of offering love to others that is already within us. The issues we grapple with leave us pondering the existence of privilege in an unequal world. We question the meaning of life and our daily choices.

I use the metaphor of diamonds when speaking of the journey of Contemplative Psychology because this is a path of building the intensity capacity (defined in chapter V) to face the trials in life. As we do so, we become more trusting of touching and living from our vulnerability. Each of us can skillfully offer ourselves to others with a heart of genuine compassion and be of enormous benefit to the world. What each of us has to provide others is unique from what everyone else has to offer. We are each a brilliant jewel in our rights—we all possess a diamond within—however, the mechanism and functioning of our mind's psychology is a mind map that we all share. Each of us has the potential to love ourselves and feel compassion for others, no matter whether we agree with them or not. We can learn to rouse genuine compassion instead of righteous anger and frustration, and this is enormously beneficial to ourselves and others in these challenging times.

I've been teaching Contemplative Psychology for 27 years through Karuna Training. This book is part memoir and part compendium to the body of work that makes up Contemplative Psychology. I have sought in these pages to make vivid and accessible the transformative magic of Contemplative Psychology, which trains people experientially to befriend themselves, be authentic with others, possess agency, and, most importantly, transmute difficult emotions into wisdom.

—Melissa Moore, June 2021

SECTION ONE

Tilling the Ground
of Intrinsic Health

CHAPTER I

What Is Contemplative Psychology?

Contemplative Psychology marries Eastern and Western psychology and encourages students to explore the paradox of the inseparability of wisdom and confusion, with meditation as a baseline practice and method by which we learn to face and touch our fears.

Contemplative Psychology is considered a path of *mutual recovery.* This orientation flies in the face of traditional psychotherapeutic training. Nowadays, many therapy approaches understand how deeply affected people are by those they work with as therapists. Mutual recovery points to the non-dual dimension of our beings, of our inseparability from others. This inseparability can be utilized in supporting another's sanity through the practice of *exchange*; however, working this way requires the practitioner to be deeply grounded and trust in their own basic sanity.

Learning the Practice

The practice of Contemplative Psychology (initially known as Contemplative Psychotherapy) was founded in the mid-'70s at the Naropa Institute (now Naropa University) by psychiatrist Dr. Ed Podvoll in collaboration with Chögyam Trungpa. Together they birthed Naropa's master's degree in the practice and seeded a body of work that this book aspires to preserve and propagate.

An eccentric man with a passionate heart of devotion to Buddhism and contemplative methods, Dr. Podvoll was adamant that, as young therapists, we must not take refuge in *therapeutic speculation.* He coined the phrase *therapeutic aggression* to call out the fascination with a psychological preoccupation with "why" things are the way they are. Instead, he encouraged us to look directly into the present moment to find everything we needed to know about those aspiring to help.

He admonished us not to hide behind psychodynamic theories and approaches. Instead, we were encouraged to be 100% present, available, and responsive to the people we served. To enter our sessions with curiosity and "not-knowing mind; without diagnosis or the trappings of therapeutic know-how." In a sense, the program was in-depth genuineness training—utilizing contemplative methods to be more authentic and as we are.

Podvoll was dramatic and entertaining too; for example, instead of simply studying Freud's Interpretation of Dreams, we wrote down our dreams nightly for months and then asked to apply what we found in our dreams to the understanding of Buddhist psychology. During the final exam at the end of the first quarter, Dr. Podvoll posed as Sigmund Freud and proceeded to interview us in small groups about our understanding of getting to know our mind through dreams. He wanted to know the merits of utilizing meditation versus dreams for introspection on our minds and how it operates. Dr. Podvoll often said, "If Freud had been introduced to meditation, he would have abandoned his work with dream inter-pretation altogether." Ed Podvoll believed meditation to be a more reliable, intimate, and accurate microscope into the working of one's mind than dreams could ever be.

In my era of training at Naropa Institute, we were not introduced to the Diagnostic and Statistical Manual of Mental Disorders (DSM) because Dr. Podvoll knew we'd immediately be indoctrinated by the pathological mindset upon entering the field. He did not want to enforce that view on us during our training. The main point Dr. Podvoll drilled into us is that there is nothing to fix. We merely provide a container within which they will discover their natural unconditional health. The therapist and client meeting is an oppor-tunity to transmute confusion into wisdom on the spot with one's unconditional compassionate presence.

The early degree programs at Naropa were unique in their approach to education, even for an experimental 1970s and '80s. Naropa was America's first accredited Buddhist college and an early institution dedicated to introducing Eastern philosophical views and practices.

The entire master's level cohort underwent a three-month Maitri Space Awareness (MSA) retreat together at the Rocky Mountain Dharma Center (now Shambhala Mountain Center) in Red Feather Lakes, Colorado. The practice is one of lying in specifically desig-nated postures in five different colored rooms, called Maitri rooms, which are each shaped differently for each Buddha family. Maitri is Sanskrit for *loving-kindness* toward oneself and others, and the practice of space awareness has to do with connecting to our natural openness—or the self-less nature of our existence. These rooms were designed by Chögyam Trungpa to induce psychological experience and space.

By the end of my first MSA retreat, I felt crazier than I'd ever been before. In the beginning, I did not know how to sit with myself, my mind, or my feelings as encouraged, and thus I acted out my emotions and indulged my many mental habits of self-hatred. My constant distractions were enacted through excessive exercising, eating disordered behavior, reading anything that wasn't dharmic in nature, writing long letters to family and friends, and constant chit-chatting. I was awarded the name the "most untamable being" by the faculty at the end of that three-month retreat. I was in good company; as I remember, others did a fair bit of acting out too. Nevertheless, along the way, I realized that no matter where I went, there I was, still acting out!

The MSA process is one of wearing out one's habits, adopting simplicity and discipline, and through some generosity toward oneself, learning to give oneself a break. I've had to repeat the lesson many times over in life. Years later, driving with a fellow Naropa graduate from my cohort, we found ourselves howling with laughter at some of the shocking incidents that had occurred during our MSA retreat. We wanted to make sure those things had happened as we remembered them because they were so extreme.

We recalled a fellow student who was a former priest and an accused pedophile hiding out in retreat in Colorado under another name. Law enforcement came to the dharma retreat center and arrested him in the middle of meditation.

Another student, an older male whose significant drinking problem had already kicked him out of the program, had come back in the night and kidnapped his former girlfriend, and then held her hostage at a local motel in Red Feather. None of us knew where she was until my boyfriend and I discovered the two of them on our day off.

In another startling event, the lead teacher of the retreat wrestled a disturbed woman to the ground in front of the shrine room during mealtime. Everyone was very silent and pristine during the meal, and the woman was standing at the shrine making invisible silent offerings as she often did, and suddenly she was tackled and hauled off. There was no explanation.

The incidents shook my faith in the methodology and its instructors. As someone who came with a little trust in the program, these incidents somehow threw me back on my strength. Eventually, I persevered, and, in the end, sanity prevailed. In retrospect, it's hard to believe that Naropa did not incur a host of lawsuits at the time, but it was the tail end of the 1970s and considered somewhat normal for the day to be unconventional. The Shambhala organization is currently embroiled in a "Me Too" incident concerning the leader, Sakyong Mipham Rinpoche; however, the root of the current upheaval began in the behavior of Chögyam Trungpa. His demeanor and that of those around him were always interpreted as sacred, no matter what. I own the spiritual bypassing I employed for nearly 40 years on the Shambhala path, and for any harm caused. I sincerely apologize for not awakening at the moment. Yet, somehow, my Maitri Space Awareness retreat became one of the most enriching and influential experiences of my life.

This exercise in communal living tended to provoke wild habitual patterns that could not be ignored. I learned to be with myself as I am, literally sitting with myself silently and surrounding my ferocious mental habits of self-hatred with loving-kindness. The main point of MSA was to engender Maitri and make friends with ourselves as we are. Reflecting on my training some 40 years ago with 2020 hindsight, I see what the program's intent was aiming for, yet that was not exactly the outcome. However, the blessings are countless.

Encountering the World of Therapeutic Aggression

Freshly graduated from Naropa Institute with my master's degree, I was hired by one of the first eating disorder treatment facilities in a for-profit hospital in the mid-1980s. I was called a Treatment Facilitator for an in-patient hospital ward in the Boulder Adventist Hospital at 4th and Mapleton in Boulder, Colorado. That job propelled me on a revealing and disappointing 12-year journey through for-profit psychiatric medicine.

Eating disorder treatment at the time was aimed at middle-class, late adolescent women from affluent America. American adolescent girls and young women were manifesting an epidemic of disorder symptoms in the form of both anorexia and bulimia. Once hired, I could not understand how I ended up in the care provider's role instead of the patient. I was working 100% with myself; honestly, when comparing myself to my clients, as young therapists are prone to, I believed the contributing history to my eating disorder was far worse than my clients' histories. It didn't make sense to me how I ended up on the "healer" side of possibilities.

My career in for-profit medicine abruptly ended once I recognized I could no longer support the misogynistic traits of psychiatry. I recognized that I had to move away from a world where diagnosis is used to stigmatize women to control them, and then blame them for their sanity in calling it out. Toward the end of my eating disorder therapist career, I was amid my doctoral study at the California Institute of Integral Studies in San Francisco.

I experienced a massive crisis of faith in the psychotherapeutic model altogether, based on my front-row seat in witnessing the ineffectiveness, misogyny, and profit-gouging approach. I had to make a radical leap out of my East-West psychology doctoral program into something new. I integrated my East-West psychology credits with studies in psychological anthropology—how culture affects behavior. I was seeking a wider lens than psychology to address eating disorders and women's psychological problems altogether. My inquiry prompted me to study women, rituals, and food as the topic of my dissertation. These studies on ritual and nutrition helped me to recognize that the atrocities being enacted on the earth are also being recapitulated in women's bodies.

This widening of my lens is what led to Karuna Training offering certification in Contemplative Psychology, as opposed to Contemplative Psychotherapy. We have not replicated what Naropa does, which is train therapists, but instead offer the view, meditation, and action of the teachings uncoupled from therapeutic application. Contemplative Psychology grows and expands the heart and sharpens the mind, regardless of if we are credentialed as a therapist. The path of mutual recovery transmutes confusion into wisdom through exchanging self with others. Thus, the journey of Contemplative Psychology is to become more selfless, open, wide-seeing, and compassionate as we go.

The journey is one of befriending and genuinely loving ourselves and eventually becoming responsive and beneficial in offering love to others. People of all walks of life need supportive people and environments of love in order to trust and tap into their vulnerability. Karuna Training is a contained safe environment that is dedicated to propagating this love. Trusting the minds of others can be a tall order in times as we live; the world we are experiencing seems out of control! Therefore, Karuna Training devotes itself to creating cohorts of sanity to support everyone who participates to discover the diamond within themselves. Everyone has a diamond within, and yet not everyone shines as they are born to do. Karuna is the environment that shines the jewels of the diamonds within us.

The Vessel of Karuna Training

Karuna Training offers participants a two-year professional certificate in Contemplative Psychology. Not designed to train therapists, Karuna is a program that is open to those interested in a contemplative approach to care. The Karuna curriculum has developed continuously starting in the mid-1990s through to present to be applicable for people seeking skills in Contemplative Psychology.

Karuna Training first arose out of my teaching seminars in Contemplative Psychology all over Europe in 1995–1996. I was in Europe as an emissary of Sakyong Mipham Rinpoche, who sent my then-husband, David Schneider, to Europe to be the Director of Shambhala Europe, and I came with the package as a Buddhist teacher. I asked the Sakyong at that time what I should be teaching and he said, "Why don't you teach Contemplative Psychology?" I began offering short weekend seminars and programs all over Germany, the Netherlands, Austria, France, and Spain, and in Eastern Europe too. Karuna emerged when five Germans[2] approached me about doing a more comprehensive training in Contemplative Psychology.

In the beginning we founded ourselves as Upaya, LTD (Upaya means skillful in Sanskrit), and they worked circles around me in establishing the organization. I focused on creating the original cur-

2 The founding members of Upaya, LTD were: Hubert Backes, Dagmar Niehaus, Lisa Fey, Gabi Gokert, and Angelika Schulz.

riculum that walked people through the Buddhist teachings experientially, and we strongly aspired to create a safe process-oriented experience that we called Karuna Training. I can say I didn't know what I was doing. I invited other faculty in; Paul Cashman highly influenced the original curriculum and Irini Rockwell for a short period. I made a lot of mistakes by not understanding the impact of such a training endeavor.

In France, I was fortunate to visit the monastery where Dr. Podvoll had gone into a lifelong retreat to ask for his blessings in teaching Karuna Training. In the half-hour we had together, he said, "Only teach people to meditate; nothing else matters." There is something incredibly kind and practical about Ed's advice, and meditation has remained central to the Karuna curriculum. Meditation is the ground of all Karuna's contemplative methodologies developed to offer participants a wealth of transformative change.

Eventually, the Karuna Training program evolved to what it is today with the guidance and stewardship of Barbara Maertens in Germany. In 2006, Barbara and I honed the curriculum into a manual to American Psychological Standards, and in North America we have been able to offer continuing education credit as a result.

Meditation is what makes Contemplative Psychology *contemplative*. Contemplative means expressing or involving prolonged thought and sometimes is associated with Christian prayer. Here, the term is used to mean joining the head and the heart. Thus, Contemplative Psychology is a practice of synchronizing the head and the heart through thoughtful, in-depth meditative inquiry.

The curriculum of Karuna Training has evolved considerably over the past 25 years. Karuna has developed its own language and innovative methodologies to transmit the complexities of the work, specifically Maitri Space Awareness (MSA), the practice of Compassionate Exchange, and facilitating groups in the non-dual space of nowness. Many of these methods are presented in this book in the context of learning and applying the practice of Contemplative Psychology.

Overview of Chapters

The first section of the book, *Tilling the Ground of Intrinsic Health*, aspires to establish the basic principles of Contemplative Psychology. The view of intrinsic health and the jewel of our Bodhicitta, or awakened heart, are unveiled. One's innate capacities, all that we already possess within, are nurtured in meditation practice by learning to stay with ourselves and be with ourselves as we are.

This section explores the Buddhist definition and mechanism of ego, with emphasis on how our ego is not the enemy. Ego, however, does cause unnecessary suffering. Learning to investigate how the ego provides a path to access the mind is taking our ego as a teacher. The path of Contemplative Psychology is one of befriending oneself first and then learning to benefit others. This section explores the origins of Maitri Space Awareness and the Contemplative Psychology understanding of the inseparability of confusion and wisdom.

The second section is called *Taking Emotions as Path*. The chapters explore what emotions are from a Contemplative Psychology perspective. This section highlights the unique way emotions become a path of awakening our innate wisdom. Contemplative methods of learning to feel feelings fully and directly as energy arises is a path of staying with our confusion. Often, as I'm teaching these ideas to beginners, it sounds like I'm asking people to stand in an electrical storm with an aerial antenna to be fried alive. There is preparation and training for tolerating the intensity of emotions, which is grounded in mindfulness-awareness meditation. How meditation prepares one to stay with intensity is a method of cultivating the capacity to remain awake, present, and open in the face of discomfort.

Through Contemplative Psychology, we discover our minds are workable and our emotions provide a sophisticated operating system to navigate our lives. Our mind, our feelings, and how we function are something we all equally share. The content within our minds and how we operate emotionally is based on our conditioning and habituated biases. What each of us has to offer is unique from everyone else. We are each a brilliant jewel in our rights; we all possess a diamond within us.

The third section, *Mining the Experience of Not One, Not Two,* draws from Zen meditation Master Suzuki Roshi's quote about the experience of the Buddhist notion of emptiness, or shunyata. Shunyata occurs when we lose the grips of ego and experience the truth of groundlessness. Shunyata is the point on the path of Contemplative Psychology when we become braver and daring. Letting go of our solid ideas and definitions of who and what we are and experiencing the non-dual nature of our capacity to exchange freely with others and the world is the primary topic.

This section explores the birth of Compassionate Exchange, learning to offer ourselves to others with the heart's genuine processed capacity. People do experience this directly, and it evokes another's basic sanity on the spot. For many years, I've witnessed hundreds of students learning to get out of their own way and recognize the potency of their hearts. Students let go of their self-consciousness and begin trusting themselves to be who they are.

The final section, *The Moment-to-Moment Art of Compassionate Exchange,* is about personal and global sustainability through the practice of Contemplative Psychology. The last section of this book explores Contemplative Psychology in an applied way to create a life that balances one's responsibilities with a sacred outlook. Creating, living, and evolving out of a sacred mandala, we ascend an invisible spiral staircase of passing through life's lessons that reveals innate wisdom step by step.

CHAPTER II

What Is Health?

By the time I found Naropa Institute's Contemplative Psychotherapy program, I was way down the rabbit hole of habits of self-hatred. I held myself hostage on the scale daily; over-exercising, binging, then restricting with food and internal harsh self-talk were the norm. Quite honestly, I wasn't interested in meditation. I certainly wasn't looking for anything slow and thoughtful, nor was I seeking a spiritual practice of any kind. The whole reason I wandered into Naropa Institute was that I could sense something exciting was happening there at the time! Allen Ginsburg, Anne Waldman, Barbara Dilley, Peter Orlowski, William Burroughs all were there. I wanted to be wherever the hip thing was happening at the time. That is the truth.

Now, in hindsight, I can say it was my *intrinsic health* that drew me to Naropa Institute. However, it was not at all conscious. It was more like I accidentally wandered into the mouth of a crocodile, and the mouth closed around me. I began to realize that no matter where I went, there I was. There was no escaping myself; I had to learn to befriend myself! Ironically, I was in constant pursuit of health, only to discover the jewel of my health was already inside of me.

By synchronizing our bodies, breath, and mind in the present moment in meditation, we can glimpse a feeling of wholesomeness, openness, and the freshness of being fully present. In meditation, we naturally come back to the present at any moment, and by doing so, we resource ourselves from within ourselves. We call this source of openness within us *intrinsic health.* Through meditation practice, we learn to resource ourselves by drawing on an open innate strength we already possess.

Contemplative Psychology is a lifelong path of trusting oneself enough to be open, permeable, and attuned to the present moment. This book will introduce us to our intrinsic health and our *awakened heart,* or Bodhicitta, both innate jewels that we already possess. Contemplative Psychology is grounded in Buddhist meditation, an ancient understanding of how the mind works and developing a discipline of contemplative awareness. By practicing the Contemplative Psychology methods introduced in this book, one gains a synchronized body, articulate speech, and an awake mind.

Through the practice of Contemplative Psychology, one gains the ability to discern what is internally generated and what is externally stimulated in our being. To discriminate between our thoughts we are thinking from what is happening in the present moment. We learn about the source of our projections on others and how to gently and radically cut through habits of discursiveness in ourselves. We not only make friends with our minds; we learn how to be open and available to the messages from our world naturally.

In this chapter, we discover an essential resource we all possess: our intrinsic health.

What Is Intrinsic Health?

Intrinsic health is unconditioned health, an innate capacity within us to synchronize ourselves with the world and all the world's wisdom in the present moment. Intrinsic health is also known as *basic sanity*, which is pointing to a natural state of health we can access within us. This unconditioned health or sanity within us cannot be corrupted or tarnished no matter what. According to Contemplative Psychology, intrinsic health is a human birthright.

Health, as a word, has been co-opted by the materialistic imprint of consumerism, which has convinced many people that health is equivalent to youth, beauty, thin and fit, being wealthy, or you fill in the blank. These notions of health are far from the innate health I'm pointing to here.

There's a journey required in rediscovering one's intrinsic health due to the false notions we've built up around ideas of health. We're distracted from any sense of possessing unconditioned health due to habits of acting out of an unsynchronized body, speech, and mind. We are often looking at a screen with one hand, possibly driving with the other, and in the back of our minds worrying about what we must do next. We sometimes glamorize that by calling it "multi-tasking" and struggle to remember what we have accomplished any given day when we are so divided in our attention and emotions—all the unembodied.

Contemplative Psychology is a journey of learning how our bodies, speech, and mind are not actually separate entities; however, to cultivate awareness, we pay attention to synchronizing all three in the present moment. By synchronizing our body, speech, and mind, we begin to contact our intrinsic health. Along the way, we become aware of habits of desynchronizing—how we are always trying to do a little bit more with the time we have and end up causing ourselves mishaps due to mindlessness. Contemplative Psychology is a path that requires befriending ourselves, no matter what. Befriending warts, horns, and claws we'd rather others not know exist. These habits I speak about are always about clinging to ideas of who we should be instead of who we are.

Even our habits arise from this resource of intrinsic health. We often think we have bad habits that once we are rid of we will be *healthy*! However, that puts our habits through a pathological lens when, in fact, all habits start because we're avoiding pain and seeking pleasure—even if it ultimately brings us more suffering, like a bear who goes back again and again to the beehive for honey. The bear seeks the pleasure of the honey to rid himself of the pain of hunger regardless of the stings, and always he receives pain with his pleasure-seeking habits. We all do that: developing habits out of a desire to seek the good stuff and taking the bad along with it. Despite the pain attached to the pleasure, we keep going back to the honey pot, back to the refrigerator, back to the wine glass, back to our empty electronic devices, etc. Most of us are ensconced in habits of seeking pleasure and avoiding pain day in and day out, and we don't stop to notice.

In modern parlance, we label this habit-forming tendency *addiction*; however, from a Contemplative Psychology perspective, addiction is merely human nature's purest expression of unmet confused desire or always involves connection-seeking behavior. There is innate health in our passion for connection; we need one another. There is health in our desire for happiness and peace. However, the methods of achieving relationships can become obstacles in and of themselves.

We all desire happiness and peace, and yet, often, the best we can do is get tiny glimpses of openness and relaxation here and there. Suppose we are present enough to open our sense perceptions to the present moment and we synchronize our perception to the world and its inhabitants. We glimpse the experiential feeling of being inseparable from the world. This ability to be present and synchronized opens us to the wonder of the unconditioned experience. We experience the magic of being present.

Being attuned to the present moment is being synchronized with our intrinsic health. Through familiarizing ourselves with habits of mind, we learn to turn our allegiance to this very ordinary experience of basic sanity. This unconditioned experience is never goal-driven; we are not hunting for it, but it automatically happens. When we are in nature, while walking, we notice a sudden shift in the air and the temperature as the seasons change from summer to fall. We fully experience the thin layer of ice forming on a pond on a late autumn morning. We notice the first bud of a crocus sprouting in spring, or we gaze into a clear, vast, starry night of July in the Rocky Mountains. We can attune to these moments in short glimpses of synchronization in our bodies, speech, and minds. When we are present with the world, we are resourced with its innate beauty and basic sanity.

The view of intrinsic health is akin to the Buddhist doctrine of *Buddha Nature,* which is the seed of enlightenment within us all.

For most of us, however, our enlightenment is obscured by our mental, physical, and verbal habits. In Contemplative Psychology, we explore the notion of intrinsic health. We do so intentionally because Contemplative Psychology is a path meant to be applied more widely than to just those who identify as Buddhist. For that matter, these methods are more widely applicable beyond being any kind of therapist or care provider. These methods attune us to our innate humanness.

Intrinsic health is a foundational pillar of Contemplative Psychology. These words define an experiential reserve within us, available anytime we are present. Inherent health is a wakeful resource inside of us that we cannot blemish, destroy, or tamper with no matter what. We often forget about our basic sanity, becoming lost in conceptual forests in our minds. Repeatedly, we become caught up in habits that distract and occupy us, habits arising from things we made up trying to make sense of pain and suffering.

Tapping into the Intrinsic Health Within

In the late 1980s, I was living in the Castro District, the gay district of San Francisco, California, when the AIDS epidemic was on fire. Before treatments became available and science caught up with the crisis, the AIDS plague was a devastating epoch. My then-husband, David Schneider, and I attended a good number of funerals for young gay men who were close friends. At the time, David was writing *Street Zen*, a book about a Zen abbot, Issan Dorsey, who founded and ran Maitri Hospice before he himself died there of AIDS in 1991.[3]

---

3 Schneider, David, *Street Zen: The Life and Work of Issan Dorsey* (Boston & London: Shambhala, 1993).

I spent quite a bit of time at Maitri Hospice and noticed something in the young men dying. They seemed to take either a right or left turn in the face of death. If they turned one way, then they were at peace with their death, accepting and radiant even—you could say, open to their fate. The other turn was the opposite, to be embittered, angry, blaming, and distraught over their fate, which nobody could blame them for, of course. I attended so many funerals at the beginning of the AIDS epidemic that I lost count and found myself cycling with fear and anxiety over the ensuing plague.

However, from a Contemplative Psychology perspective, those choices (along, of course, with an infinite array of other choices) are available for us in every moment. As I got to know the dying men along the way, I realized the defining difference was whether someone could be present for what was happening in death, synchronized with their fate, and open to the consequences. I realized those individuals were in touch with their intrinsic health, even as they were dying. Meanwhile, others struggled to synchronize with the present circumstances of their life, keeping them out of touch with the intrinsic health they also possessed.

We all are challenged to synchronize with the present moment. We don't feel right, we don't like the circumstances we are in, we feel hurt and disappointed about several issues. Nevertheless, living with chronic illness and pain makes it challenging to be synchronized. All those things and more can be true and still not disrupt our connection to the absolute reality of our intrinsic health. These expressions of emotion and frustration need attention, love, and care. However, no matter what, we still have our basic sanity. We still possess our unconditional intrinsic health.

Intrinsic health is prevalent and accessible anytime. Our inherent health prevails ceaselessly whether we have a diagnosis that proves we are certifiably crazy or are dying with a terminal illness. This reservoir of sanity within us is a resource from which we learn to draw from daily. Our basic sanity is a conduit of wisdom. Intrinsic health gives human beings access to the world's wisdom because we are never separate from the world, even though our minds can convince us otherwise.

Strangely, the wisdom of the world doesn't belong to us. This kind of wisdom is self-existing. It is something we automatically tap when we are present and synchronized in our body, speech, and mind, meaning we can access our unconditional sanity. When we synchronize our actions, our emotions, and our awareness in the present moment, we attune to the world's wisdom. We glimpse the world's basic sanity because we and the world are not separate.

The world's wisdom promotes the changing of the seasons, the ebb and flow of the tides in the ocean, the sun's rising every morning, and the cycles of the moon, the stars, and the planets in the galaxy. Nobody is turning on a switch for all that to happen. There is innate rhythmic wisdom arising out of basic sanity, available to us as inhabitants of this magical world we are co-inhabiting.

Human intelligence and human sanity are not separate from the wisdom that displays itself daily in the world; however, as a species, we've come to believe we are separated from the world's wisdom. Possibly we think we're smarter than this wisdom. As a species, we've developed dangerous beliefs that we possess more wisdom than the wisdom of the world, which has led us to the current state of affairs of ecological devastation and climate change. These beliefs have caused devastating results for humans and many other species.

This ecological disruption is a wake-up call for us to recognize our insignificance and, at the same time, our responsibility as a species in the play of things. Every time we watch the latest weather fiasco or natural disaster, we could wake up to our interconnected nature with the Earth's elements and all its inhabitants. Intrinsic health has to do with this reservoir of wholesomeness and unconditional appreciation for life everywhere and shared.

One could say the entire path of Contemplative Psychology is about attuning to one's own and the world's intrinsic health so that we become beacons of basic sanity in these challenging times, for our own sake, for others, and the world at large. In this way, we begin to trust ourselves and the world, regardless of the ripening scenarios in our lives in the present moment.

CHAPTER III

Uncovering Intrinsic Health
with Meditation

M editation is not a discipline that I came to easily. Though I was proudly named The Most Untamable Being by teachers at Naropa, for me, learning to meditate was more like roping a wild bronco. It was an arduous task to ask myself to sit quietly with myself in the present moment.

Once I was introduced to meditation, I realized quickly that I didn't like the empty time of not doing anything and sitting with myself. It was difficult, tedious, and sometimes painful. All I experienced, in the beginning, was an edgy feeling of anxiety. I hold deep compassion for those who struggle with getting themselves to the meditation cushion because establishing a meditation practice forces us to be in touch with ourselves as we are. It took me eight years to establish a consistent and committed practice of meditation.

In this chapter, we are introduced to the fundamental meditation technique that will experientially connect us to basic sanity. We explore the primary point of practicing meditation, a specific method designed to support the discovery of our innate health. We're opening to the experience of being who and what we are, as we are.

We've learned a lot about the effect of trauma on the experience of meditation since I was learning to meditate in the late '70s. We now know that there are many people for whom meditation is impossible at first. People who have trauma in their bodies, hearts, and minds, and are too anxious to sit with themselves in meditation, are quite common. I believe that was true in my case, but I was fortunate enough to soldier through it. I did so with a lot of seasoned support from meditation instructors. I was ensconced in the heart of the Vajradhatu community of Chögyam Trungpa in Boulder.

We now know asking people to sit down and bear it until the anxiety subsides is not always the most effective way to learn meditation. Sometimes the only thing we can do is to synchronize our bodies to the present moment through walking mindfully, yoga, or an embodied practice. Some sort of embodiment that synchronizes our movement with the breath gradually appeases the nervous system enough to settle into simply sitting and breathing.

Meditation is nevertheless a worthy path whatever way we may meet on the cushion. It's about learning to relax and self-regulate with who and what we are. And, as we do so, we are naturally accessing and attuning to our basic sanity. Intrinsic health occurs naturally when we synchronize our body, breath, and mind in the present moment. When we are fully and unequivocally here, attending ourselves and the world without a watcher, without the self-consciousness of holding ourselves present artificially. This is an experience of being present to ourselves and the world as it is instead of how we would like it to be.

It is common to be unsynchronized in the present moment; often, we're doing one thing with our bodies, like driving while talking to someone else on the phone, and in the background worrying about what we must do later in the day. This multi-tasking, now a prized skill, is often believed to be mandatory to navigate the perils and fast-paced everyday life demands. Yet our multitasking attempts, which split us into compartments, only serve to disconnect and separate us from the font of intrinsic health within us.

Unfortunately or fortunately, depending on our nature, it means we must slow down, and we must slow down a lot! The best way to discover one's intrinsic health, though perhaps not the only way, is through regular meditation practice. In meditation, we learn to synchronize our bodies, our breath, and our minds in the present moment. Mindfulness-awareness practice exercises the muscle of mind to come back to the here and now, again and again, and again and again and again.

I'm prone to saying, "The only problem with meditation is that you have to do it, and you have to do it a lot." Like anything good, it takes time. Our relationships take time to ripen into friendships, as grapes take time to mature into good wine. In meditation, we are strengthening our mind's muscles to be present with ourselves as we are, not as we want ourselves to be. It takes time to sit and be with ourselves and learn to be as we are. That is what we are practicing—just being.

Meditation takes bravery and discipline, and along the way, we learn to accept and make friends with ourselves. That is the practice—befriending ourselves as we are—instead of launching into meditation as a self-improvement project or a notion of trying to be something we are not, like "calm," "peaceful," or "open." We do not sit down on the cushion and suddenly become a calm person with the cool of a Zen priest. We might feel like a screaming meanie, a rageful mom, or a disconcerted heartbroken partner, or whatever else we are that we wish we could change; that is who shows up.

In meditation practice, the main point is whatever we find in ourselves now, we make friends with energy. That's why meditation can be so tricky. We are not changing ourselves; contrary to common mindfulness approaches, we are befriending what is.

Mixing Mind with Space

In becoming a meditation teacher, I learned there are two kinds of beginning meditators; one type sits down and receives some sort of meditation instruction. The first time they attempt to meditate, they are like "ahhhhhh space . . ." For this type of meditator, space is an instant relief. The other kind of practitioner sits down the first time, feels into space, and instantly freaks out. This type of person is actively avoiding space. But this is also a manifestation of their intrinsic health, protecting them from what is too painful.

Meditation is about relaxing your mind into space. No matter what kind of mediator we begin as, making a relationship to the porous and obstructive nature of space is part of the journey. Space is the mind's natural makeup, so when we try to examine our mind, experientially, we don't find much unless we are using machinery and are wired up to a PET scan of some sort. We cannot find anything of real physical substance in our mind, except thoughts.

However, despite its intangible nature, our minds also can affect everything about our moment-to-moment experience. The mind has potency. This non-substantial thing called "mind" is made of space. In meditation practice, we learn to relax our mind's inner space with the world's outer space. With time and practice, we get a glimpse into the notion that there is no separation between inner and outer, except boundaries we've self-imposed.

Space is one of five elements in the Tibetan categorization of elements: space, water, earth, fire, and wind. Space is the central, most pervasive element from which all other elements arise out of and dissolve back into, so it's monolithic as an element.

In meditation, we are mixing our minds with the world's space. Space is potent and pregnant with all kinds of energetic feelable potential instead of being empty and dull. Space is like the ancient Anasazi cliff dwelling sites, empty but apparent that something went on there. We can feel something amid the nothingness of space. That is what is meant by the pregnant potential of space. In Contemplative Psychology, space is always our starting point. What is coloring the space right now? When we sit down and learn to meditate, we are taking a temperature of the space of the present moment.

We study and learn about all the elements in Contemplative Psychology and that all the elements can be contorted and have many faces to them. As is true with the openness and malleability of space, at the same time, we can employ the element of space to dull our mind, ignore the present moment, and blanket our awareness. Space is the densest of elements and can make us "spaced out" experientially. There is always a continuum to discern when studying the elements physically, psychologically, and spiritually.

Beginning a Meditation Practice

Meditation is the baseline practice of Contemplative Psychology and is what makes Contemplative Psychology *contemplative*.

Contemplative, here, means the timeless experience of synchronizing with the present moment in our body, speech, and mind.

The meditation technique recommended for this is formally called *Shamatha Vipashyana*. It is adopted to Contemplative Psychology as a foundational method that underlies and informs all the other practices we impart in Contemplative Psychology. It's essential to start your meditation practice if you plan to work with other Contemplative Psychology practices yourself.

Meditation practice is attuning to the space of the present moment with mindfulness and awareness. The technique is sitting in an upright posture, either on a cushion or a chair, and feeling grounded and rooted on the earth, with the feet on the floor or folded legs. The important thing is that we experience an uplifted sense in our torso with a sense of permeability and strength simultaneously. We are relaxed and awake.

In this approach, we meditate with our eyes open. We keep our eyes open as a proclamation of being awake to who, what, and where we are, as we are. We sit upright, breathing, and learn to rest our mind on both the in and out rhythm of the breath. We feel the breath, and that is our anchor to the present moment. The breath is the object of our meditation, that with which we are synchronizing our mind and body.

Sitting and breathing, inevitably we will find that we are thinking too, which is only natural. We are not trying to rid ourselves of thoughts; that would make us dysfunctional. However, we are practicing not to be ruled and captured by our thoughts. So we can regard our thoughts like the ticker tape at the bottom of the CNN broadcast. When we try to read it, we cannot keep up with and understand the commentators simultaneously. So we practice gently disregarding and allowing that ticker tape just to run, as our thoughts run on, carrying on in what Chögyam Trungpa called "subconscious gossip."[4]

Meditation allows our thoughts to dissolve eventually; with time, they wear out their potency and their rule over us. But again, it takes a lot of meditation practice and a substantial relationship to space, which involves extended periods of practice.

When my meditation instructor first suggested I go on a solo meditation retreat, I dutifully booked a week in a cabin at Dorje Khyung Dzong in Gardner, Colorado. I must confess that it didn't go so well, as I tried to corral myself with the practice. I rigidly set up a schedule and wanted to pour myself into it, which didn't work. In the middle of the retreat, I managed to run off—literally. I discovered the hippies living next door at a commune and managed to hang out and get stoned with them for a couple of days before completing my week of retreat. That was a dramatic exit and challenging for me to ignore the display and habit of escaping myself with entertainment and drugs.

I was only one year into my Naropa master's degree at the time, feeling somewhat slammed by my craziness after a long three-month retreat in that program. I had broken up from my necessary and constant boyfriends and was working hard to relieve myself of the habits of marijuana consumption. It took many years to understand the intrinsic sanity that marijuana played in my youth as self-medication. I forgive myself for that necessary self-medicating habit now,

---

4 Trungpa, Chögyam, "Consciousness" in "Glimpses of Abhidharma" from *The Collected Works of Chögyam Trungpa, Volume 2* (Boston & London: Shambhala 2003), pp. 285–286.

and at the same time feel grateful to those who embrace cannabis as medicine for anxiety openly, now 30 years later.

We are and will continue to be confronted with the task of holding sight of our intrinsic health, a view of primordial purity. We learn to do so in the face of our own and the world's insanity again and again. There is a significant difference between sanity and insanity—they're not the same. Insanity causes harm, either blinding us to ourselves or others' pain and suffering. Basic sanity brings humility and insight, warmth, and compassion for the world's confusion and provides us a path forward.

In Contemplative Psychology, we understand that basic sanity is our birthright. Thus, Contemplative Psychology is a lifelong journey and path of accepting ourselves as we are, entirely. After that and along the way, we learn to offer ourselves to others as a vehicle of intrinsic health. When we meet others with recognition of their basic sanity, they can feel it. It feels like a healing balm for the woes of the world.

How to Practice Mindfulness Awareness Meditation

When first learning to meditate, it's helpful not to expect results but to be curious about what is going on experientially while we are meditating. The method is more about how we administer the technique rather than doing it right. We are practicing applying a kind of non-judgmental inquiry into our mind and to our relationship to space, which is what we encounter when we sit in silence. We're making friends with ourselves, not trying to fit ourselves into an established form. Feel free to experiment with the suggestions offered below.

For those of you who are more experienced in other meditation techniques or yoga, the suggestions below are offered as a gentle inquiry into how you experience your mind in the present moment. When you can detect a difference in the effect of your meditation techniques, you are cultivating a refined awareness. At some point, it's helpful to commit fully to one method, but not strictly.

In either case, we're feeling into the experience and methods suggested until we find some ownership of them, meaning they fit our nature and support being present and relaxed. Meditation is a vehicle to discover our inherent health. We are practicing synchronizing our body, speech, and mind in the present moment. Relaxation usually occurs when we wear something out, thus the more friendly and inquisitive we can be from the onset, the more we will discover.

Note: Meditation instruction is better to receive, or at least review, in-person from someone with experience in this specific technique. There are several meditation teachers through Karuna who are available for such training.

Still, there are some basic instructions you can follow to get started with a meditation practice on your own.

1. **Set up a conducive environment:**

    It is important to meditate in an environment that is clean, quiet (if possible), and tidy. Since, in this technique, we keep our eyes open, it helps to have a focal point that is meaningful, like an altar, flower arrangement, or window through which to gaze. If we try to practice in a messy or noisy environment, or places like our offices with technology present and so forth, we will only think about what we must do next and/or be frustrated by the distractions. The point is to practice meditation in a space within which we can relax and let go of our to-do list.

2.   **Decide on the amount of time you will practice before you begin:**

It is easy to get into meditation and suddenly realize how overwhelmed and busy you are and think you don't have time to sit in silence. If we can dedicate 10 minutes to begin with, then 20, then 30 minutes, we build the capacity to sit with ourselves as we are.

3.   **Take your seat:**

Find a comfortable and upright posture on a cushion or chair. Make sure there is a sense of uprightness, head balanced naturally over heart, heart balanced over the hips. If we can sit comfortably cross-legged, make sure that the knees are lower than the hips, or you will have pain in the back. If sitting in a chair, then it is important to have both feet anchored on the floor. You can use the back of the chair to support yourself but try not to slouch.

4.   **Take an upright posture:**

Meditation can be practiced sitting, walking, lying, or standing. However, there should be a sense of being upright with the natural curvature in the back. Your shoulders, jaw, and tummy are relaxed. Take time to do a body scan at the beginning or several times throughout the session. In this practice, one moves with awareness slowly across the body, usually from toes to head or head to toes, in order to feel if you are holding tension anywhere. Then breathe into any tension spots and relax the tension consciously. Some tension doesn't melt easily so notice that—it's information about your body.

5. **Allow yourself the space to land:**

Feel into the contact your body makes with the earth. Feel the sense of uprightness and openness in your torso. Just sit and feel your body sensations, sense the temperature in the room, and sense the feelings and energy within you without trying to figure out the reason why. Whatever you meet, practice non-judgmental awareness. The kindness of just noticing.

6. **Eyes are open, loosely focused:**

One of the unique aspects of this technique is that the eyes are open, the gaze is down five to six feet in front of us and loosely focused, meaning we are not looking at anything. We can widen our gaze and take in the whole environment simultaneously. Many people learn to practice meditation with their eyes closed, which is a different technique with different results. This specific technique is about being awake and present. If we're someone who has learned to meditate with our eyes closed, it's good to alternate back and forth to experience the difference for ourselves. Practicing with your eyes open strengthens your mind more to work with the distractions, situations, and circumstances in life as they are.

7. **Attune to your breath:**

The breath is the object of meditation; once we settle down we simply anchor our awareness on the breath. The breath is a natural anchor to the present moment and something to come back to when the mind wanders again and again.

8. **Attune to the out-breath and feel into space at the end of the breath:**

    Once we learn to utilize the breath as an anchor to the present moment and an object of meditation to be present, then we specifically attune to the out-breath and feel into the experience of space at the end of the breath. This takes time. Emphasizing the out-breath in meditation is a gesture of letting go. Feeling and touching into space at the end of the out-breath is specific to feeling into our innate openness and intrinsic health.

9. **Notice your thoughts but don't follow them:**

    In meditation, we are strengthening our mind to be present. The mind naturally wanders, and its vehicle is thinking. If we notice we are thinking, we are already back in the present. We simply feel into the flavor of our thoughts and find the breath. We learn to allow our thoughts to occur without following them. This is advanced and takes time. So as a beginner, we don't need to give ourselves a hard time if we get lost in thoughts; it's natural. That is why we are meditating, in order to notice the experience of being present and the experience of being away. We are taming the mind to be present, and that takes lots of kindness and relaxation.

10. **Sit, breathe, and feel your body and the environment:**

    We have nothing to accomplish, and the main point is to relax with whatever we are feeling. Dropping out of the head and into the body is an excellent way to give space to the mind.

11. **Repetition and practice is the key to meditation:**

Meditation takes time and repetition. That is why we call it practicing meditation, as we are practicing being with ourselves as we are. Some days are easier than others, and over time we learn to ride the ups and downs of our moods, emotions, and restlessness.

CHAPTER IV

Ego Is Not the Enemy

I remember when I realized there was no way to get away from myself; I was a 25-year-old student and beginning meditator. I'd already undergone a severe wake-up call during the three-month Maitri Space Awareness retreat in the mountains of Colorado, part of the Masters in Contemplative Psychotherapy program at Naropa Institute. During the retreat, my classmates and the faculty had cared enough to intervene with me about my progressed eating disorder behavior. I'd been cycling through bulimic rituals on the retreat, and people had noticed. I was told I had to seek therapy for my problem to maintain enrollment in the program. It was an effective intervention, but it had not been my choice, so I did not immediately integrate the severity of the problem.

I remember the moment vividly. I was standing outside of a 7-Eleven convenience store right after consuming a pint of Häagen-Dazs ice cream, familiar with my pattern of binging on ice cream and then purging before the substance can digest. It was a sunny Sunday morning; I'd already gone for a run first thing that morning. I knew sitting meditation was being offered in the meditation hall of Karma Dzong in downtown Boulder. I knew I could go there and sit with the consequences of eating ice cream. My therapist and I had been talking about that as an option; "sitting with the consequences," she had said. I decided to try practicing meditation and sit with it, as it was.

I still recall every moment of that morning's meditation, the push and pull inside of myself to vacate myself (of my crime). *"But what was the crime?"* I had to ask myself as I sat there. I had merely overeaten, but with the intention of purging. I felt how sitting with myself was more kind than purging. I could recognize that sitting would make me less likely to binge in the future, and that was the last time I binged and purged. Unfortunately, it was not the last time I binged, but I've learned to sit with the consequences, quite literally.

Gradually, through meditation and learning about the natural capacities of mind, I could see how twisted I'd been and how undermining of myself I was in my beliefs and habits of mind. I could see that there were many more options and space to have more agency and choice. Learning about meditation's effect on the mind became very helpful because I could experience the different capacities of my mind and see how I was applying them. I became curious about space and how to experience it without trying to fill it. Through meditation and studying the ego's mind map, I began gently taming my destructive habits and rituals. Contemplative Psychology's journey is about befriending ourselves and the everyday challenges we experience in turning our allegiance again and again to intrinsic health.

This chapter explores the development of *ego* from a Buddhist perspective and how understanding the Contemplative Psychology mind map of ego supports an understanding and experience of *fluidity* or *unbound openness*. Fluidity means that we are emotionally and energetically ever-changing, dynamic, and permeable. And unbound openness is the discovery of space as a natural state within us. When we experience openness, there's no hint of self-consciousness or any trace of being preoccupied with ourselves. The alternative to fluid unbound openness is to be frozen in our habitual tendencies, nurturing beliefs of who and what we want to be, imprisoned by the thoughts of our conditioning.

Social media offers us an excellent example of how our minds are continually regurgitating our thoughts repeatedly, to create a sense of continuity and concrete notions of who we are. Ideas like, "I was simply thinking about buying a winter coat and, suddenly, coats are populating my virtual stream . . . hmmm." Our thoughts become more solid when we are refed our algorithmic clicks and interests over and over. The nature of thinking mind is similar in utilizing the same emotions and beliefs. Take politics, for example, always conditioned by our experiences and repeatedly rerun in the culture around us. The mind replicates itself to know that it exists. Understanding ego's working as an apparatus will help in learning not to believe everything we think, which is what we are practicing in meditation. The ability to disengage from thinking mind, when we want to, is a huge step in the process of learning to rule our minds.

Understanding Ego from the Perspective of Contemplative Psychology

Habitual tendencies can be distilled into one word: *ego*. Ego, as defined in Contemplative Psychology, is how we assure ourselves that we exist. It is *how we know* who and what we are from moment to moment. This knowing is our mind generating assumptions about a made-up repetitive construct of habitual thoughts and solidified ideas. For example, it can be how we identify and tell the story of our history, how we understand the storylines of who we are and why we are the way we are, our ego's storyline.

In this chapter, we define ego from a Contemplative Psychology perspective and learn how to approach our habitual tendencies with *maitri*, or loving-kindness. Cultivating maitri means nourishing a sense of unconditional warmth and kindness; it means making friends with the parts of ourselves that we usually judge. Maitri is the bedrock on the path of Contemplative Psychology. Befriending our egoic tendencies, but not necessarily buying into the storyline, is how we make friends with ourselves as we are. Ego is merely our concrete ideas of identity, and ego is only problematic when our identity gets challenged.

The study of ego lays out a mind map of how ego maintains itself. Understanding how we maintain our ego is directly correlated to the liberation of ego. To apply Contemplative Psychology, we must understand the Buddhist mind map. Becoming intimately familiar with the mind map of ego, not just theoretically but also method-ologically, allows us to release fixed ideas of who and what we are on the spot. Our mind map is made of space infused with thinking, emotions, projections, opinions, interpretations, and fixed views of consciousness. Thus Contemplative Psychology offers us a compre-hensive mind map of how ego functions.

Letting go of thinking is, of course, strengthened in meditation practice, when we see we are thinking and gently, but firmly, bring ourselves back to the present moment. When caught in our own beliefs and definite ideas about reality, it is not easy to cut through thinking and drop into the present moment. Learning to feel into the body, speech, mind, quality, and action of the current moment is truly a skillful means of unequal discipline. Letting go requires genuine trust in intrinsic health and the strength of mind to trust open space or *egolessness*.

I've been teaching about the mind map of ego in Contemplative Psychology for many years, and it's usually met with a fair amount of resistance. I've gone through periods of wondering if I'm inept at presenting the material or if it is so dry and specific to start with that it's hard to land. I have learned over time that the ego doesn't like to study itself. Ego's glue is ignorance. It's like we are the last ones to see ourselves trying not to be ourselves, and yet our habits and styles are on full display for everyone else to see.

Ignorance, desire, aggression, pride, and ambition can all be used as fuel for the ego's engine. These raw human emotions are, again, innately healthy in and of themselves. Yet, like everything else, when we group our feelings altogether in the act of defensiveness to protect an idea of who we are or who we think we should be, then we have a defended fortress of "self." We end up creating a self that works against itself, fighting with the world to survive. From a Contemplative Psychology perspective, intense conflictive emotions are the ego's defense mechanism to survive. We could say they are an alarm system.

From a more extended perspective, the ego is the cause of suffering in and of itself yet becoming familiar with the ego's mechanisms and understanding its defenses is the discipline of becoming familiar with the mind's movements. The more aware and nuanced we are about our mind's activity, the more we are on the path to liberation. That is just one of the paradoxes of Contemplative Psychology. Learning about the ego's mind map is already learning too much to keep the ego's illusion in play. We can no longer ignore that we are the driver of this manufactured self. And no matter where we go, there we are! There is no getting free of ourselves if we are truly paying attention.

We learn the ego's mechanism to befriend our ego tendencies, and through acceptance, we wear these ego tendencies out and liberate ourselves in the process. The emphasis in Contemplative Psychology is more on how we approach ourselves instead of striving for a result. Contemplative Psychology is a path of cultivating openness with a precise awareness of the present moment. Eventually, we become skillful and kind in our actions. First, we learn to apply this toward ourselves and our habits; then, we learn to offer ourselves to others as a space of nonjudgmental awareness. In the journey of discovering that which we already possess, we can cultivate trust in our intrinsic health as a resource for resilience and strength when things get tough.

We need the strength of mind to look directly into our challenging habits of mind, to be kind, forgiving, nonjudgmental, and curious toward ourselves. Contemplative Psychology encourages us to befriend ourselves, to make friends with that in ourselves, which we tend to degrade the most. These habits of mind are what we use to maintain an illusory narrative about ourselves, the habituated *beliefs in* and *beliefs about* ourselves, such as "I'm not good enough," "I don't belong," or the opposite direction, "I'm the greatest person on earth." Wherever we fall on the continuum of self-consciousness, either praise or blame, to own those and see them for what they are is a way of deconstructing our habits of mind and cultural conditioning.

Contemplative Psychology does not deny the truth of human suffering. We embrace it and study it first within ourselves and then through deep listening to others. Contemplative Psychology's approach toward suffering and pain is to be curious, nonjudgmental, open, and friendly toward our experience. We call this *maitri*, which, as noted earlier, translates from Sanskrit as *loving-kindness*. It is a necessary ingredient when learning to tolerate the sensations of difficult emotions and painful energetic experiences without fleeing. Our capacity to stay with the energy strengthens our minds. It sharpens our *intensity capacity* to stay with whatever we don't like as we seek to access strength of mind.

All human beings seek pleasure and avoid pain, and there is intelligence in doing so. We're conditioned to believe that our habitual tendencies, destructive behavior, or addictions are the real problems. In Contemplative Psychology, however, we aspire to be curious about these habitual tendencies, both within ourselves and externally reinforced. When we can be genuinely nonjudgmental toward our habits of mind, we are planting the seed of compassion. Curiosity helps us to cultivate a compassionate and nonjudgmental presence when we meet these same habitual tendencies in others. Ultimately, Contemplative Psychology is about exchanging skillfully with others, but the first step is to befriend ourselves as we are.

Skandhas: The Building Blocks of Ego

The Buddha taught that ego is the cause of suffering because of how we cling to notions and ideas about who we are, but the world doesn't always confirm our egoic construct. It's interesting to meet and listen to time-separated siblings tell their story of being raised by the same parents; their experiences are usually quite different from one another. It's almost like other parents raised them, but that is due to how the parents changed with time, how their consciousness changed with each sibling. The editor of our personal histories is ego, and the salvation from solidity is our capacity to change. According to Contemplative Psychology, the ego is a dynamic construct, and it reconstructs every 1/160th of a second.

Internally, we share the same capacities of mind, unless there is biological, neurological, or traumatic injury; however, we rarely share the same experiential content or tell the story the same way. These shared capacities of mind have movements and can be named and identified. However, it is essential to understand how the mind's capabilities that create the ego are also the stepping-stones to our basic sanity. From a Contemplative Psychology perspective, it is essential to study these capacities of mind nonjudgmentally because the mind that traps us is the same mind that wakes us up!

We call these capacities of mind *Skandhas*, a Sanskrit word meaning "heaps." We construct ego from Skandhas, which are fragments of experience that we coagulate to create ideas of who we are. The five Skandhas are the building blocks of the ego. Skandhas are five capacities of mind that we all share. However, the mental content and nature of the experiences are all unique to us as individuals. There is no central headquarters within us, which we might believe is the "thinker" behind our thinking mind. From a Contemplative Psychology perspective, we merely connect the dots of our experience and create a story, making us feel more reliable and secure than we are. The ego is a mechanism of protection to make us feel assured that we exist.

The most exciting thing about the Skandhas is how fast they happen. Skandhas are a repetitive mental mechanism that we use to reconstruct our sense of self in every new instance. Like a flipbook of cartoons, the moving pages appear as if they are animated. The same thing is happening for our sense of self too. There are many gaps in our solidity of self, and thus we need to reconstruct our idea of who we are again and again.

This act of reconstruction is what makes our minds habitual. Imagine when we are doing the same task repeatedly; we find a path of least resistance and do things the same again and again. Thus, Skandhas are the mind's way of reconstructing ourselves over and over. It happens so fast that there is no gap; however, the process is full of holes and open to change. The gaps in our egoic construct are what save us.

Chögyam Trungpa said, "If you have a body, you have Skandhas."[5] So, even in an enlightened state of consciousness, these aspects of the mind are operative, although perhaps they are not so speedy and can be seen through. Understanding each Skandha for its experiential movement is one way to befriend our Skandha process. The Skandha process is said to be fully developed by the age of eight, and Skandhas are habituated through experiences in our developmental years, along with the *karma*[6] we brought with us into this life. In Karuna Training, we intentionally avoid the question of rebirth, so central to the Buddhist religion, in order to make the material more accessible and ecumenical. However, it is important to note that the mind map of ego includes the imprint of what we bring from previous existences, what the Buddhists call karma.

---

5 Trungpa, Chögyam, "Consciousness" in *Glimpses of Abhidharma, The Collected Works of Chögyam Trungpa, Volume 2* (Boston & London, Shambhala 2003), pp. 285-286.

6 Karma—the Buddhist doctrine of interdependent origination; illustrates the cause and effect of how habitual patterns replicate themselves from lifetime to lifetime.

These concepts can be difficult to grasp cerebrally. Here are descriptions of the nature of each Skandha, followed by a table aimed at offering a simple and easily comprehensible view of what they are and how they operate with one another. Skandhas are a primary element of the mind map of how we know we exist.

The First Skandha

The first Skandha, or capacity of the mind, is called "form." Trungpa Rinpoche named this Skandha "first split" to describe the origin of duality from our natural interconnected nature. This capacity of the mind is experienced like a birth, which arises out of openness or space. We are resting in space, undefined, and suddenly there is a flash of self-consciousness caused by anything external. This split is very faint and primarily undetectable, but it is the birth of "this" and "that," or "me" and "that outside." The first split is the birth of conscious duality, like the first time an infant notices "mama" as something separate. The experience of this is a very, very subtle capacity of mind and not substantial enough to confirm that we exist, so we engage the other four Skandhas as reinforcement.

The experience of the first Skandha is one of shock. We are going about our business, dreamily, lost in a fog and feeling merged with space and carefree. Then an email or post appears in our mind stream, either literally or virtually in our thought, and suddenly we are split into turmoil and despair. We feel separate and consumed when we feel this kind of disturbance. Our world is suddenly disrupted, but we usually can't identify fully without adding many other capacities of mind to make us more solid in our despair.

The Second Skandha

The second Skandha is the "feeling" Skandha. This capacity of mind occurs on a pre-verbal level and is subliminal in its experiential nature. The second Skandha is how we continuously feel into space or others to detect whether we feel safe, unsafe, or neutral. This mind capacity can be particularly disturbed when we grow up in environments where it's not safe and there is neglect and/or perceived or actual violence. Unsafe environments result in subliminal trauma, often unconsciously experienced whether or not there is a true threat. A continual feeling of being unsafe becomes habituated and is applied randomly to multiple experiences. Still, the feeling capacity, or second Skandha, isn't enough information to ensure that we entirely exist.

The Third Skandha

So we engage the third Skandha, or capacity of mind called "perception." Trungpa called it "perception-impulse" to describe its reactionary quality. This capacity of the mind is a bit sharper and more decisive. We can discern the experience of others as to whether we like, dislike, or feel neutral toward our experience. A reaction formation arises from this Skandha, which propels us toward experience, away from experience, or into apathy. This Skandha habituates around reactions of accepting and rejecting our experiences.

We experience this capacity of mind anytime we are discerning whether we like something or dislike something. For example, while shopping, we think, "I like this. I want this. It fits me," or "I don't like this. It's not right." This discerning aspect of the mind is continually and habitually picking and choosing experiences out of liking and disliking. Still, this capacity is not strong enough to confirm our existence, so we engage the fourth Skandha.

The Fourth Skandha

This Skandha is called "intellect," where we have the capacity of the mind to name and label experiences. I feel "happy," "disappointed," "appreciative," or "despondent." This conceptual capacity is fully conscious and the place where the mind becomes genuinely habitual. There are 50 or 51 *samskaras*, which are conceptual habits of mind that act to define our experience repeatedly. We share these samskaras or patterns universally but experience them differently and individually, depending on our individual development. The samskaras are what color our personalities, each one unique but made from the same ingredients. However, the fourth Skandha is as much of a made-up construct as the rest of the mind's capacities in confirming who and what we are.

The Fifth Skandha

Finally, the fifth Skandha is called "consciousness," which holds the entire mechanism of our egos together. Consciousness is a solidification of the other four Skandhas into a sense of who we are, what it feels like to be us, who and what we like and dislike, how we experience phenomena, and who we believe ourselves to be. All this gets recreated again and again every nanosecond within our minds. Consciousness is the mind's operative functioning and how we make sense out of our experiences and navigate our worlds, skillfully or not.

The fifth Skandha is understood as the Eight Consciousnesses, each consciousness of which has a capacity of mind that solidifies into a solid sense of self. Each of the first five consciousnesses of these eight is related to a sense faculty, such as the eyes, ears, nose, tongue, and mind. The sixth consciousness is the mind. The thinking mind has a consciousness of its own. The consciousness of sight, hearing, smell, taste, touch, and thinking mind can be experienced in the present moment, and thus are easily experienced through the practice of meditation in a contemplative environment.

The seventh consciousness, known as the afflicted consciousness or what Trungpa called "cloudy mind," utilizes ignorance, doubt, and fear to co-opt the first six consciousnesses into the notion that "I do exist . . . because I see it, I smell it, I taste it, I thought it," etc. It is known as the afflicted consciousness. It meets the present moment, which the eighth consciousness generates out of our past experiences, and co-opts all the other consciousnesses into solidifying me, myself, and I.

The eighth consciousness is known as the store-house consciousness. From a Buddhist perspective, the eighth consciousness holds all the seeds of whatever one has thought, felt, or done in numerous lifetimes (if you adhere to the notion of rebirth) or in this one lifetime. An infinite number of karmic seeds ripen when the causes and conditions are right in this life. Karmic seeds are the material by which the seventh consciousness integrates the five Skandhas into generating "I am," and "I exist" every 1/60th of a second.

This material is not easily digested, and again the ego does not like to be studied. Later in the book, I link the five Skandhas to the five Buddha Families, as is traditional in the Vajrayana tradition of Buddhism. Studying the five Buddha Families is key to experiencing the subtle movements of mind and how these capacities of mind are co-opted by habitual patterns into our everyday life experience of who we think we are.

8 Consciousnesses—the map of the fifth Skandha is the dualistic consciousness	
1st Consciousness of sight	The first five of eight consciousnesses are operated through the senses. All the Skandhas are interdependent, and consciousness pervades them all; none of them could function without the presence of consciousness, so it's already inherent in the first Skandha of form. Form is the bare existence of the sense and their objects; the fifth Skandha brings it all to life, as it were. Consciousness relies on all the other Skandhas in order to operate. It is not a fixed entity, nor some abstract state of pure consciousness, but an impermanent, changing, and dynamic process.
2nd Consciousness of hearing	
3rd Consciousness of smell	
4th Consciousness of taste	
5th Consciousness of touch	
6th Mental Consciousness	Equivalent to thinking mind. It coordinates the input from the other senses and experiences thoughts and feelings. Everything that comes through the senses from outside and all the ideas and emotions that arise from within reach us as mental images and serve as objects of the mental consciousness.
7th Afflicted Consciousness	Responsible for our sense of self. Trungpa called this "cloudy mind" because it is clouded over by ignorance, the fundamental emotional affliction. It is the pain of not knowing our true indestructible awakened being—our intrinsic health. This ignorance permeates the consciousness of the six senses so that all our perceptions are immediately influenced by confusion. Also, a link between the first six consciousness and the eighth consciousness.
8th Base Consciousness/ Alaya—Vijnana	Trungpa called the eighth consciousness the "storehouse of reference points." The eighth consciousness acts as the basis of the other seven as a memory bank. It is drawn on from the seventh consciousness to mix with the experience of the first six consciousnesses to fortify and reinforce our version of reality, which is all about "me." The eighth consciousness is what holds the imprints left by past experiences that, in turn, become the seeds of future experiences. It is diffuse and undifferentiated; it is not even dependent on a body and this lifetime.

The five Skandhas and Eight Consciousnesses are also how and why we change over time or even in a flash. The change of consciousness is possible because the construct of our conscious selves is fabricated and porous, full of gaps and holes, and constantly changing.

The basis of one's intrinsic health has breathing room in this permeability structure. Our innate openness and the gaps in the Skandha process support our health; without this permeability to consciousness, we would be in permanent states of mind, which would prove insufferable. Imagine being in a bad mood forever and never getting out of it. Some people habituate solid states of mind and suffer deeply and are diagnosed with clinical disorders. However, even with the diagnosis of a clinical condition, there are gaps in our states of mind, and we can touch and taste our innate openness.

Befriending Our Mind

In Contemplative Psychology and through meditation practice, we learn to experience the mind as fluid and ever-changing. The same goes for our ideas of who we are and who others are, which change equally. When we meet people and decide suddenly that we don't like them but are not sure why, usually we are in a habituated projection on the person. Similarly, we can like someone a lot initially and sometimes project a kind of perfection on them. Then, when their true nature begins to be revealed, we can be let down that they don't fit our perfect pictures.

Holding the understanding that our narratives are pieced together out of the five Skandhas, pieced together again and again from fragments of experience, helps us befriend our ego's habitual aspect. We can become familiar with ego trends and begin to see how we apply the same trends in multiple situations and cause ourselves a lot of suffering. For example, if we believe that we deserve a certain kind of acknowledgment or attention from others socially, when that acknowledgment doesn't come our way, our ego feels discontent. That feeling of being ruffled, and dissatisfaction, become habitual and begin to be applied to all circumstances, even when acknowledged.

Our ideas of who we are bump up against all kinds of challenges every day, whenever the world is not meeting our expectations. We develop habits of condemning the world for not meeting our expectations, or another direction is to create an ego that believes we are undeserving of acceptance. It doesn't matter whether we are a confident construct of self or a wounded construct of self, our egos cause us suffering if we believe solidly in who we are and what we think is true.

Despite this, our egos are not the problem. The ego is not the enemy. We are called on to have some sense of a self in the world to sufficiently function. The world expects us to have an identity and continually asks us who, what, and how we are. The problem, if there needs to be one, is the habituated aspect of ego. The habitual and unconscious mechanisms of the mind are causing us both pain and a lack of knowledge about how the whole apparatus works within us. Understanding and investigating each capacity of mind that makes up the five Skandhas is the Contemplative Psychology path. The ability to see through it and drop out of ego-fixation and into the present moment is the method of Contemplative Psychology. Getting familiar with the mind and its multiplicities' capacity is the practice of Contemplative Psychology.

Mindfulness awareness meditation is the baseline approach to becoming familiar with and making friends with ourselves. Each capacity of the mind that is engaged in the five Skandhas can be uncoupled from the prospect of creating an ego. Then, that capacity of mind becomes a path to liberation. Meditation practice is the process of sitting with ourselves for extended periods and becoming familiar with the mind's capacities.

Maitri, or making friends with oneself as we are, is the stepping-stone to compassion. It means making friends with our survival mechanism, which is ego's game, or resurrecting someone in ourselves that we must learn to protect. Befriending ourselves to develop maitri is a necessary step on the journey of living with a compassionate heart.

Some folks try to skip over the befriending of oneself, and they get a lot of burnout as a result. From a Contemplative Psychology perspective, compassion fatigue isn't possible; the "burnout" provider's experience is due to the struggles in protecting one's own heart from pain that has not been integrated with love and gentleness within oneself. Otherwise, when we are genuinely friends with ourselves, we can bear witness to all suffering in others because the heart's capacity is bottomless. When we have not done our homework, so to speak, and approach ourselves with maitri, we end up using the act of caring and we try to solidify ourselves in the role of caregiver or someone who is needed. This kind of caretaking is challenging to maintain because it's not entirely the truth, and we are seeking confirmation from our acts instead of giving selflessly.

Compassion is the translation of another Sanskrit word, *Karuna*. Compassion here means we can experience another's pain inseparably, thoroughly, and entirely. Living an engaged, compassionate life is the aspiration of studying and practicing Contemplative Psychology. Some believe meditation is a practice of ridding oneself of the ego, but from a Contemplative Psychology perspective, we aim to understand and befriend the ego instead. The ego is not the enemy, and this isn't a path of disowning ourselves. Instead, understanding the permeability of ego and the mind's capacities is one step on the journey of being more of who we are.

CHAPTER V

Openness Is Our Natural State

There is wisdom in everything. Even when we cannot discern it, the self-existing wisdom is there. We've all had the experience of seeing something completely different in the present from what we thought was happening when the event was occurring. With time and space, we gain a greater perspective on our interpretations of reality, our feelings change, our understanding evolves, and we feel differently in the long run. We change our minds about people, events, and complicated emotional situations.

A deeper understanding of both how our mind functions and what conditions our perceptions comes into play in the path of learning the mind map of ego in Contemplative Psychology. As we know theoretically, the mind clings to ideas of who and what we are to survive. We also realize the effect of the ego's survival game on ourselves and others experientially. We are studying the nature of the mind's habits and their impact on our lives and relationships.

This chapter explores how we know we exist and what marks our existence without ego's constructs. The Skandha process described in chapter II is driving our narrative. In Contemplative Psychology, we understand that our life narrative is a construct. We embrace our story as a confabulated tale threaded together with fragments of experiences, which we react to, interpret, and then solidify into "who we think we are." However, our personal experience is all we must work with, as we currently understand it. Our lives are an experiential portal to the mind map of ego. This chapter is about rousing maitri, or loving-kindness, toward ourselves and our habits of mind. When we can practice maitri, we develop true equanimity.

The Three Marks of Existence

We spent the last chapter investigating how we don't exist in a reliable, impenetrable way or in the way we habitually think we exist. We link Skandhas together to create a narrative that virtually ignores the gaps in our story and strings together a solid idea of who we are. Then we are tasked to defend that idea of ourselves. Defending our ego-identity leads to lots of kerfuffles, disappointments, and even tragedies because the world doesn't always agree or go along with our confabulated narrative.

In Contemplative Psychology, there are three ways we all share the marks of our existence; traditionally, this is Buddhist teaching known as the Three Marks of Existence. We could call them "the three truths about our existence that we all share." We share these truths equally, meaning class, race, or socioeconomic factors do not alter these truths for anyone. However, how we experience and live these truths depends on our cultural and familial conditioning. It means our view and acceptance of these truths is the most significant factor in how we experience them.

The first mark or truth of our existence is that human beings suffer! Humans suffer just by being born in a human body. Birth itself is intensely painful for both mother and child, even though we celebrate new life. Our human conception's guaranteed sufferings can be summarized into four categories and applied physically and metaphorically: birth, old age, sickness, and death. These four experiences come along with the territory of being human, like a curse that comes with a castle. We cannot bypass these four passages no matter how hard we try or how much money we try to throw at them.

These are the baseline sufferings: birth, old age, sickness, and death. And then there are the sufferings that we create by attempting to avoid these baseline sufferings. The ways we resist change or any new beginning or birth, the ways we cover over aging and pains of growing older, the energy we spend, and ways in which we avoid sickness and deny death. All these are secondary kinds of suffering, unnecessary suffering that arises from avoiding the unavoidable. Contemplative Psychology discerns what type of suffering we are experiencing, always guiding us to come back home to ourselves as we are and investigate what we bring to any given situation.

The 1993 movie *Groundhog Day* best depicts the endless cycle of how we all habitually avoid the truth of suffering. Bill Murray plays a reporter stuck in a loop, reliving the same day. The character learns by making different choices each day, and, over time, he becomes smarter about how to navigate the obstacles that he's repeatedly presented. The movie reveals how much easier it is to be kind, accepting, open, and generous to our experience than to try and manipulate our experience into what we want it to be.

We are all living the same day over and over, because wherever we go, there we are! We have multiple opportunities every day to meet the truth of suffering from a place of openness, kindness, and awareness versus trying to manage and manipulate our experience into our version of what we want it to be. On the Contemplative Psychology path, we learn to discern the kind of suffering we are experiencing, baseline suffering, or unnecessary suffering due to our inventions.

The second mark is that nothing lasts, everything dies, and the entire world and all experiences are impermanent. Impermanence characterizes everything—every blue sky, every tear we cry, every difficulty we face, every accomplishment we make, our moods, emotions, minds, relationships, washing machines, appliances, homes, favorite toys, etc. They all fade, die, and eventually vanish. When we fall in love and then find that we can't hang onto the good times, when we have a new car and it gets its first little ding—whatever it is, we can't hang onto the newness. When we feel or think negatively about another person, we can't hang onto the resentment either, not without a lot of effort and energy.

Learning to lean into the truth of impermanence as a mark of our existence is a key practice in Contemplative Psychology. Just consider whether anything lasts, and it's impossible to identify anything that is not in flux. Change, decay, and death are the nature of everything.

Once, I was conducting an exercise, and I wanted to use an extended meditation gong tone and continue for 10 minutes. I wanted a gong tone to last so that participants could sit with the gong's tone for an extended length of time and use sound to feel through all the changes that arise, but I could not convince the gong to comply. In the end, I gave up the exercise as I was driving myself crazy. The truth of impermanence defeated me.

We find ourselves chasing our tails, continually trying to make things last—the romance, the party, the high, the success, the freshness of something new. Eventually, everything becomes used, worn out, dated, and ultimately dissolves into space. Everything physical, emotional, and mental is forever evolving, changing, and dying. Even mountain ranges, oceans, galaxies, and entire universes are arising and dissolving right before our eyes. And thank goodness! Imagine if everything stayed the same; we could appreciate nothing! It is essential to contemplate personally, embrace, and make friends with the inevitable truth of change.

The third mark of existence is that we're not as stable and dependable as we think we are. Ego is a construct made of those heaps of experiences—Skandhas—and there is no *there* there! The whole construct we call "me" is full of holes and gaps. It is like a dream we piece together using "secondary revision," Freud's name for the way we fill in the narrative of a dream so that it makes sense.[7] In Contemplative Psychology, we learn not to fill in our storyline but to experience the gaps and eventually claim them as our natural openness. Those holes and cracks are glimpses of the third mark of existence, called *egolessness*, or the experience of no-self.

The egolessness experience occurs in flashes when we are not maintaining a solid idea of who and what we are. However, when we lose our reference points too quickly without a foundation of understanding, this experience can be terrifying. Emptiness, or in

---

7 Secondary Revision—a Freudian term used in *The Interpretation of Dreams* to speak to the way in which people have dreams that are missing information and then we fill in the gaps to make them make sense. The material is all coming from the mind, so it's all considered legitimate for interpretation from a Freudian perspective. Freud, Sigmond: *The Interpretation of Dreams* (New York: Perseus Books Group 1955), p. 68.

Sanskrit, Shunyata, is the Buddhist word for egolessness. I find the word *emptiness* very misleading, and I prefer to use instructor Judith Leif's phrase, "unbound openness." "A more accurate translation of shunyata would be 'unbound openness.'"[8] Meditation that leads to the experience of shunyata involves letting go of mental supports and letting in the fresh air. In unbound openness, we experience ourselves as we are—present and open. This openness is our natural state and is the resting place of our intrinsic health in Contemplative Psychology.

Building Intensity Capacity

As we continue to learn about the mind map of ego and descend into exercising the muscle of being with ourselves as we are (instead of who we think we should be), we acquire the skill to investigate in the present moment contemplatively. We do this by feeling what and who is here in the present moment. We find it is ever-changing; isn't that a relief?

The ability to tune into our own and others' suffering altogether without a narrative and the ability to feel pain directly is an acquired skill in Contemplative Psychology. The skill is the ability to recognize and touch the truth of impermanence—to see, inquire, feel, and accept the reality that nothing lasts, and embrace the open moments of relaxation when we can touch and mix our minds with space. Usually, this happens after a lot of meditation, sometimes on a walk in nature. That openness is our natural state.

---

8 Lief, Judith, "Shunyata & Linguistics I" from *Speaking of Silence: Christian and Buddhists in Dialogue* (Halifax: Vajradhatu Publications, 2005), compiled and edited by Susan Szpakowski, p. 136.

Ignorance is the glue of the ego's mind map, and ignorance means we are proficient at ignoring reality when it's staring us in the face. Ignoring is a way to fool ourselves into seeing a cohesive narrative of ourselves and who we are, the strong beliefs we hold on to construct this storyline. The impetus of ignoring is bypassing the three truths of our human existence. However, to not bypass or ignore requires that we stay with the intensity of what is arising and not try to manipulate it.

Through the practice of meditation, we develop *intensity capacity*, which is the capacity to tolerate complicated reactions and experiences when they arise and not ignore them, but instead feel them as they are. The ability to feel through extreme circumstances in life is embracing the truth of suffering, impermanence, and that we are not as reliable as we think we are. In meditation, we practice the art of "staying with" our experience *as it is* versus how we want it to be. This "staying with" experience is how we glean insights into our habits of mind.

Many of us know the tossing and turning that can surface in the night when our lives present circumstances that we don't want. The middle of the night is when we have the least resources to meet life's challenges churned up in our minds. The antidote, from a Contemplative Psychology perspective, is to learn to feel versus think our way through life's problems. However, to drop out of our heads and feel our experience fully, we need to be embodied and practiced at feeling ourselves in the present moment. This practice takes a lot of intensity capacity and is at the heart of the journey of Contemplative Psychology.

In meditation, we exercise the mind's muscles to return to the present by feeling the out-breath. The exercise is one of dropping out of the head and into the body. We may resist this when the feelings we find in ourselves are unpleasant. But by practicing being with ourselves in the present moment as we are, we build and strengthen our intensity capacity.

For some years, I worked as a therapist on a crisis team. I was the director of a short-term safe house in Woodland, California, for people with acute mental challenges such as schizophrenia and bipolar diagnosis. During those years, I carried a pager. I was attached to this device, with brief breaks, for what seemed like eons. What I learned to do when the pager went off was to take a deep breath to presence and center myself in my body for the inevitable intensity that I was about to address. I genuinely believe I could not have handled the job without the practice of Contemplative Psychology because when the pager went off, it meant crisis. I also think that the pager and the job increased my intensity capacity.

In meditation, when we notice we are thinking, we are already back in the present. The instruction is to return to the out-breath and specifically feel the space or openness at the end of the breath. Letting go of mental activities is returning to our natural state. It's like making a physical commitment to stay present. We are not bypassing the thoughts; we simply tune into the atmosphere of mind our thoughts leave us in. For example, when we are worried about something or agitated during meditation, we don't have to dwell on the topic in our mind, which generally serves to cook up more anxiety. Instead, we can aerate the agitation and worry with space, with the out-breath.

The capacity to drop out of the head and into the body and feel our state of being is beneficial, and for many people, it is a brand-new experience. We are trapped in our heads with our thoughts and concerns and forget there is an alternative to that experience. Meditation is a practice to aerate our minds. With eyes open and attuning to the out-breath and space, we build our intensity capacity to sit with problems that perplex us. Intensity capacity allows us to feel the atmosphere of our mind without reacting or suppressing the feelings that come along with our concerns.

Again, the only problem with meditation is that we must do it! Meditation is a practice of patience, tolerating boredom, and being generous to sit with ourselves, when sometimes, we are the last person in the world with whom we want to be. This approach to meditation cultivates a nonjudgmental awareness or equanimity in us. As Chögyam Trungpa said, "The wisdom of equanimity, imbued with generosity, sees all situations equally as ornaments of basic being."[9]

Developing Equanimity

Equanimity, or "nonjudgmental awareness," is the ability to hold our own or another's experience in the space of equality. When we view our experience with equality, we can balance the natural polarities of life. How love and hate abide together, how competition and admiration co-exist, both consciously and unconsciously. We don't cherry-pick the good experiences we approve of and disregard the rest; we hold both with equal respect. This equality with our experiences requires we become familiar with our emotional and energetic habits so that we no longer feel we need to manage them.

---

9 Trungpa, Chögyam, "Visual Dharma: The Buddhist Art of Tibet" from *The Collected Works of Chögyam Trungpa, Volume 7* (Boston & London: Shambhala, 2004), p. 278.

Eventually, with practice, we're no longer embarrassed by our egoic reactions; we can see them for what they are—only habits of mind. This skillfulness occurs in degrees and takes time and a lot of meditation practice of being with ourselves as we are. We recognize our shared human habit of ignoring, reacting, and interpreting ourselves and others with humor instead of disdain. We make friends with ourselves and other patterns versus judging them.

The first degree of developing the skillful means of nonjudgmental awareness is noticing we are judging ourselves or judging another. When we see that, we learn to feel the sting of that judgment arising from ourselves. We own it. Judgment has a cynical and arrogant cast to it. Learning to see this impulse in our minds is an aspiration not to judge our own or another's experience. Once we train ourselves to notice, we can cultivate a more curious and inquisitive approach to these strong feelings. We locate the energy in our bodies, where it hits us. At the same time, we may still be nursing a narrative, and thus, it's hard to be in touch with our nonjudgmental energy. When our minds are tame enough to simply drop out of the head to feel our judgmental energy in the body, then we simply keep with it, investigating it thoroughly, joining it entirely through feeling. And because judgments are also dynamic and impermanent, through feeling our assessment, we allow it to change or dissolve naturally.

Life is continually handing us problems to solve. Depending on how we engage our daily challenges, those problems can add up, and we quickly feel overwhelmed and daunted. Human problems are ceaseless—the water gets turned off in the house, the dog swallows a needle, our kids act out, there's a pandemic, a war, or an event where suddenly we must alter our entire daily routine. There is no end and never will be an end to everyday challenges. Fortunately, they, too, in and of themselves, are always impermanent. So one skillful means of working with our judgmental reactions and struggles on a day-to-day basis is cultivating equanimity.

When it comes to evolving into the jewel that we are born to be, we are forever in a symbiotic process of outer circumstances meeting inner awareness. These two things combine to offer us opportunities to wake up and befriend ourselves. For example, we come upon a body of teachings that move us, find a book that speaks to us, listen to a podcast, or meet someone who tells us about their experience. That is an outer circumstance, which evokes in us a recognition that what we are hearing is true for us too. We identify with the external experience.

To hear those auspicious pointers in life, we must be humble, open, and available to recognize them. That means we must consider ourselves not above it all or too important to listen; we must be available. We consider ourselves equal to whoever or whatever is delivering the message, and thus, we let it in. The world is in constant communication with us if we are available. Contemplative Psychology is a journey of becoming available to the world and its messages.

Equanimity, or nonjudgmental awareness, is a skillful way to meet challenges in life. When we feel challenged and things have added up, and we can find ourselves in a fit, in those moments, evoking equanimity is remembering that openness is our natural state. Daring to raise our gaze and take in a tree, a flower, a child's smile, a cat stretching—it doesn't matter what brings us present and outside of our narratives. We can pull ourselves out of ourselves in a way to induce space and evoke this equanimity.

The ability to notice, stay with, be be kind to, be open to, and let go of our mind's reactions are an embodiment of equanimity. Cultivating this nonjudgmental awareness toward our experience is a primary exercise of Contemplative Psychology, and through this discipline, we begin to trust our intrinsic health.

CHAPTER VI

The Mandala of Now

There is a potent moment in time we mostly miss; it's called NOW! Chögyam Trungpa coined the word *nowness* to capture the present moment's potency, and he pointed to nowness as the essence of meditation. "Some people may misunderstand the term nowness and take it to refer to whatever thoughts happen to be in their mind at the moment," he contends. "Nowness should be understood as being the primeval insight . . ."[10] From a Contemplative Psychology perspective, nowness is the only place we have access to the truth of experience directly, the quintessential essence of what is present and what is true for us right now.

Learning how to attune to the space of the present moment through the potency of nowness is a foundational method of Contemplative Psychology. Of course, our habits of mind condition our experience of nowness, and it matters whether we are fearless enough to rest in *nonduality*. Resting in nonduality is the same thing as tapping into the nonreferentially of open space; the unbound openness of our existence is accessed only in the present moment. We experience

---

10 Trungpa, Chögyam, "Maha Ati" in "Mudra" from *The Collected Works of Chögyam Trungpa, Volume 1* (Boston & London: Shambhala, 2003), p. 371.

non-duality naturally when we are relaxed and raise our gaze to see the vast horizon, the moon, and stars at night, or whenever we're able to let go of subconscious preoccupation with ourselves. In Contemplative Psychology, we cultivate nondual awareness through our relationship to space.

To enhance the discovery of nondual awareness, Contemplative Psychology utilizes the tantric tool called the Mandala of the Five Buddha Families. Many may be familiar with the notion of a mandala, as it has variations in cultures across the globe. Mandala is a Sanskrit word meaning "circle" and is prevalent in Tibetan culture as a representative symbol used both for meditation and art, with deep symbolic meaning illustrated within it. The Five Buddha Family Mandala is an ancient Tibetan Buddhist Nyingma meditation tool that divides the world into five styles of being. It is explored in detail a bit later in this chapter. For now, let's consider that the term mandala, defined by Chögyam Trungpa, literally means "association society. It is a way of looking at situations in terms of relativity—things exist interdependently, and the interdependent existence of things happens in the fashion of orderly chaos."[11]

Mandalas are an ancient meditation tool that Chögyam Trungpa introduced to Westerners. He established the practice of Maitri Space Awareness (MSA) in 1970 utilizing the Mandala of the Five Buddha Families to help us explore our perception of space and nonduality. Through MSA, we gain the potential to evoke awareness beyond duality. Through the view of MSA, we are coloring in our understanding of intrinsic health or basic sanity by refining our relationship to space in nowness.

---

11 Trungpa, Chögyam, "The Razor's Edge" in "Mandala of Unconditioned Energy" from *The Collected Works of Chögyam Trungpa, Volume 6* (Boston & London: Shambhala, 2004), p. 314.

In designing MSA practice, Trungpa was evoking a skillful way to work with psychological issues. He aspired to approach the problem as an environmental issue instead of delving into developmental or specific trauma from the past. "According to Buddhist teachings, although we acknowledge that people's problems may have been caused by their past upbringing, we feel that the way to undo problems is to cultivate that person's Maitri (loving-kindness) on the spot. This is done by working with the person's immediate environment rather than by delving into his or her past . . ."[12]

This chapter introduces how to cultivate a nondual refined and nuanced awareness of space, thus turning one's allegiance further toward intrinsic health or basic sanity. The practice of MSA helps us discern the experience of basic sanity versus its opposite, which is confusion at best and madness at worst. Resting in the natural play of paradox is essential in Contemplative Psychology, which means cultivating a nondual perspective, meaning a "both/and" versus an "either/or" approach. This does not mean we deny or bypass the pain of suffering, genuine tragedy, general wrongdoing, or evil; however, those experiences are never our entryway. In the words of Chögyam Trungpa:

> *"Buddhist psychology is based on the notion that human beings are fundamentally good. Their most basic qualities are positive ones: openness, intelligence, and warmth."*[13]

---

12 Trungpa, Chögyam, "Creating Environments of Sanity" from *The Sanity We Are Born With: A Buddhist Approach to Psychology* (Boston & London: Shambhala, 2005), p. 146.

13 Trungpa, Chögyam, "The Meeting of Buddhist and Western Psychology," Prelude from *The Sanity We Are Born With: A Buddhist Approach to Psychology* (Boston & London: Shambhala, 2005), p. 8.

Attuning to Nowness

The present moment is mostly missed through mulling over the past or through wondering what the future will bring. It is *this* moment, and *this* moment alone, where we have access to the link between past and future. There is continuity between past and present, and we discover what that continuity is by attuning to the direct and fresh experience of now. We often look for how we feel and who we are through contemplating our past; however, from a Contemplative Psychology perspective, everything that is important about history we experience *right now*.

As Chögyam Trungpa explains, "according to Buddhist teachings, although we acknowledge that people's problems may have been caused by their past upbringing, we feel that the way to undo problems is to cultivate that person's maitri on the spot. This is done by working with the person's immediate environment rather than by delving into his or her past. Buddhism does not use the Western analytical approach of tracing back to the roots of neurosis in a person's past . . . Buddhist psychology works with cultivating good behavior patterns, rather than trying to analyze the person's problems."[14]

In nowness, everything we need to know is available and present, depending on how refined one's awareness is. An example is that if we carry trauma, which many of us do, it is experienced and understood within the body. We're often triggered by an external event in the present that serves to wake up the past trauma within us. If we have not explored those experiences and sensations or know nothing about them, these triggering events are confusing and leave us feeling bereft.

---

14 Trungpa, Chögyam, "Creating an Environment of Sanity" from *The Sanity We are Born With: A Buddhist Approach to Psychology* (Boston & London: Shambhala, 2005), p. 146.

From a Contemplative Psychology perspective, we can access the experience of trauma in nowness. We do so through attuning to the body and learning to hold pain compassionately, without agenda, and without perseverating thoughts that may retraumatize us. Most importantly, we do so with maitri and space.

When I've launched a new two-year cohort of Karuna Training, and we're all sitting around in a circle on opening night, I've often said, "Look around the room. Every relationship that matters to you is present in the room because you're in the room. You've already consciously or unconsciously decided who you like and who you dislike. I challenge that! In Karuna, we discover everyone has a jewel within them. Karuna Training is about shining our innate jewel and bringing out the luster in one another. We accomplish this through our relationships with each other."

My opening night comment is rarely understood at the outset of Karuna Training. Still, I've had several participants tell me toward the end of their two-year training how provocative that comment was and how it made them realize their unconscious habits of accepting and rejecting others for no reason. Then they tell me that, indeed, the person they viewed either favorably or negatively was their son, their father, or their mother energetically showing up and projected on another person.

The potency of nowness reveals how interconnected we are in this world. Through nowness, our perceived separation, the individuation we insist on to know that we exist is shown merely as ego's game. Ego is perpetually fortifying boundaries between us and the world through habitually conditioned acceptance and rejection. This dualistic splitting of ourselves and the world serves to disconnect us from the very source of sustenance we find through realizing the interconnectedness we share.

The need to know we exist is the illusory play of ego, whose job it is to divide and define us from the greater whole. When we are not separate from the greater whole, we are forever and always interconnected with others and the world. This interconnectedness can become an experiential knowing that binds us directly to our intrinsic health.

We can train our awareness to experience the infinite interconnectedness of our existence. We quickly understand that everything is dependent on causes and conditions to bring all phenomena into reality. For example, a paper towel we use to wipe a spill is interconnected to a tree, which connects to the soil, sun, water, seed, lumber company, lumberjack, parents of the logger, technology, the economy, the truck that halls the trees, the oil that fuels the trucks, the drilling of oil, mechanics, the tire of the truck, more trees, etc., etc. All of this exists in a simple paper towel. Contemplating each object's interconnectedness is a way of stimulating a sense of *interconnected knowing,* which helps us not take anything or anyone for granted in this interdependent net of connection.

Interconnected knowing can be subtle, often arriving through the ordinary experiences of everyday life—feeling a part of something bigger than us, belonging to the world, whether that be a football team, a clique at school, a sorority, a race, a wink with a friend, a political movement, or a religion. The sense of belonging is psychologically essential to our experience of basic sanity. Even if we have rejected belonging as a statement, that too portends to the importance of belonging, so much so that it must be renounced.

This kind of knowing arises from a brisk breeze hitting our face in winter, the sun on our backs in summer, the first hit of chill in autumn, and the first bud of spring—all familiar and ordinary experiences that, when fully experienced in nowness, serve to awaken a feeling of interrelated belonging to the rhythms of our world.

Through touching into the space of our interconnectedness, we evoke basic sanity.

The Birth of Maitri Space Awareness

In early 1971, Chögyam Trungpa and Suzuki Roshi, the founder of the San Francisco Zen Center, befriended one another as two influential teachers, both occupied by landing Buddhism in the West. They discussed how many of the American students showing up at their respective centers displayed serious psychological challenges of one sort or another. They promised one another they would integrate contemplative practice and Buddhist psychology to bring people home to their innate basic sanity.

Unfortunately, later in 1971, Suzuki Roshi died. Chögyam Trungpa was heartbroken upon hearing the news of his death and reflected again on their shared commitment. Trungpa Rinpoche, at the time, was teaching an advanced seminar, and he noticed that when one of his students was "acting out" with drunken behavior at a party, the space in the room began to shrink. "Little J.M. was dancing and singing his Tahiti (a kind of dance), and he wanted all of us to sing and dance, and nobody would cooperate with him. I felt very uncomfortable at the time because somebody might complain downstairs . . . then there was a world outside and above us. I felt there would be a complaint from above and below and all quarters . . . I felt very claustrophobic, and at the same time, I enjoyed his company and his beauty. Suddenly, I realized myself in a box. All those complaints and paranoid ideas and everything . . . I suddenly remembered the bardo retreat techniques for relating with space . . ."[15]

---

15 Trungpa, Chögyam, unpublished transcripts of the Second Maitri Conference, Boulder, February 1973.

Chögyam Trungpa drew from the extensive meditation training he'd undergone in Tibet as a Tibetan *Tulku*.[16] In 1972, he founded the Maitri Psychological Group with the dual purpose of first helping students explore the nuance of space and learn more about their mind; secondly, to create a community that could serve people suffering from psychological issues.

The Practice of Maitri Space Awareness

Trungpa designed five maitri rooms, one for each of the corresponding Five Buddha Families. There are specific meditation postures one takes—all of them on the ground but some on knees, some lying flat on the belly, some lying on one's back. Specific instructions for placement of arms, hands, and legs. And there are alternative postures for access needs, too, of course. These postures are held for a designated period of time, usually not more than 30 minutes. After the posture, part of the practice is to *aimlessly wander*. Aimless wandering is an important component because while lying in the postures, working with your mind—or more likely, spacing out or sleeping—it is difficult to know what is influencing us in terms of the Buddha Family. People do fall asleep, of course, in this practice, and that is not admonished; it is held as "just information!" Maitri Space Awareness practice is a great indicator on how stabilized one's mind is in meditation because the practice is very open.

Aimless wandering is walking around preferably outside in nature, without an agenda. It is part of MSA when practitioners can begin to refine their awareness by sensing the texture of their mind after

---

16 Tulku—a recognized reincarnate person who is the keeper of a body of teachings belonging to a specific Tibetan Buddhist lineage.

doing each Buddha Family posture. They look at their mood, their impulses, their engagement with the world, etc. This kind of open inquiry breeds a more refined awareness, refined with space and mindfulness-awareness. The purpose of aimless wandering is relaxing into what is and simply being and seeing what you do.

The practice of Maitri Space Awareness is done either alone in these five rooms in a rotation or these postures can be taken in meditation in a group using the same colored glasses, with everyone doing the same corresponding posture the same day. In this way, the group invokes that particular Buddha Family energy together in community; however, how that Buddha Family manifests in each person is specific to their conditioning.

The maitri postures were drawn from ancient Tibetan *Chod* [17] practices Trungpa accomplished in Tibet when he was much younger. Chod practice is an ancient Dzogchen Buddhist method where practitioners take a posture and hold it unwaveringly, usually in a charnel ground. [18] The postures can be difficult to hold, and yet they all relate to space in the way that exaggerates that Buddha Family's hang-ups. The Buddha Family postures serve to intensify one's relationship to space. However, when the postures are too demanding for some practitioners to access, then the energy of that Buddha Family translates through the group to the individual who cannot take the posture. Maitri has never been researched in

---

17 Chod—a spiritual practice found primarily in Nyingma and Kagyu forms of Tibetan Buddhism. Traditionally classified as an Anuttarayoga Tantra. Also known as "Cutting Through the Ego," the practices are based on the Prajnaparamita Sutra.

18 Charnel grounds—Tibetan burial grounds usually on mountain sides where corpses are left to deteriorate on their own. In the open air, thus called "sky burials."

scientific mindfulness labs; however, it appears that the postures and the colors are what evoke the particular Buddha Family energy in us.

Originally when Trungpa was alive, there were only maitri rooms, where people practiced alone in these postures. In the early 1990s, MSA teachers[19] figured out how to make the practice more mobile by creating a group practice using these same postures with five colored glasses.[20]

MSA works best as a group retreat practice, utilizing the experience of others in conventional dualistic comparison to begin to grasp the multidimensional aspects of the greater whole. In my own original MSA program in the 1970s (which stretched out over a couple of months, and we only had access to the postures in the rooms), I confess that toward the end, I was just going in those rooms, curling up, and sleeping. Still, the energies of the Buddha Families were getting intensified within me and were visible in the group too.

Chögyam Trungpa summarized that what we label as psychological problems in the West are, in fact, issues concerning our relationship to space. For example, we often consider ourselves solid and the surrounding space to be empty and open; however, from a Contemplative Psychology perspective, we're the porous, empty

---

19 Acharya Allyn Lyon—a Shambhala-authorized Maitri Space Awareness teacher who first instigated utilizing five different colored glasses in the practice of Maitri Space Awareness at the Hamburg Shambhala Center in 1995. It was the development of these Maitri glasses that allowed Karuna training to occur outside the walls of Naropa University, or away from the Maitri rooms. It should be noted that these are two distinct practices: alone in the rooms or practicing Maitri Space Awareness in a group using the colored glasses—both convey the energy of the Buddha Families, though differently and in varying degrees of intensity.

20 The Maitri glasses were a variation on the theme of what Chögyam Trungpa birthed; however, Karuna Training has always utilized the Maitri glasses to practice Maitri Space Awareness.

phenomena, and space presents itself as unmovable, speaking energetically. For example, when we learn the news of somebody's death, that death begins to permeate space in such a way that we cannot deny it. That is a gross example of how space is tangible. There is nothing there, yet the space of death is non-negotiable. Leaning into the solidity of space with natural openness and permeability evokes sanity. Trungpa came up with the term "space therapy" for this contemplative method.[21]

The practice of Maitri Space Awareness ripens an ability to hold paradoxes with a both/and perspective versus an either/or point of view. Holding contradictions in equanimity is mandatory to discover our own and others' innate, intrinsic health. The world is never black and white, all good and all bad, or one way or another. There are multiple truths at play in an interconnected mandala of energetic opposites and likenesses.

We have been taught that there are at least two sides to every story. Both wisdom aspects and confusing aspects abide in every psychological situation. The links between the psychology of a noble firefighter and a destructive pyromaniac are facile; both are fascinated with fire, for one thing. There is a connection between police psychology and the psychology of people with criminal intent, as both

---

21 The community Chögyam Trungpa, founded to work with others, initiated the birth of the Five Buddha Family Maitri Rooms. This therapeutic community that came to be called Windhorse, however, was an endeavor that became too difficult to accomplish for those students who he appointed to be care providers. The practice of Maitri Space Awareness (MSA) moved to the newly founded Naropa Institute in Boulder, Colorado, purposed to train the Contemplative Psychotherapy students beginning in 1974. MSA has remained a vital component of the master's training until now at the Naropa University Contemplative Psychology program. MSA is the centerpiece and has been a primary exploration in Karuna Training since its inception in 1997.

are drawn to power. And psychologists and the people they diagnose as "mentally ill" have a common focus on the struggle to achieve healing. There is a psychological continuum of space and experience that stretches between the paradox of opposites, between this and that, which points out the interconnected play of nonduality.

Have you ever considered that our greatest weakness is our greatest strength as well? How the very issues that challenge us about ourselves are, in fact, the same seeds of our greatest strengths? For example, the way we hesitate and doubt ourselves can also display itself as thoughtful strength, discernment, patience, and intelligent reserve. Or the way we boast and swell up with arrogant pride becomes humbled reflective confidence. When we consider and feel the psychological energies driving our learned behavioral habits, there is a continuum of strengths and challenges, both positive and negative influences. These interconnected reflective practices become an exercise in cultivating nonjudgmental awareness and maitri.

Another example of an interconnected continuum is whether we're more of a thinking-type person, someone who tends to lead with analysis and logic, versus a feeling-type person, someone who leads with emotional reactions and strongly feels emotions associated with every experience. The thinking-type style has its strengths, as well as the feeling-type. The thinking-type approach brings cool clarity and logic to emotional situations, which is, at times, extremely helpful, but at other times may result in emotional detachment and coldness. Overly emotionally demonstrative people also carry the asset of heartfelt expression so often missing in thinking-type people, but they may get lost in their emotions and lose their ability to think clearly at times. In both cases, the source of these individuals' biggest strengths and biggest weaknesses are one and the same.

Maitri Space Awareness teaches us to tune in to this aspect of reality, by discerning and understanding the wisdom behind five distinct psychological styles. This, in turn, fosters nonjudgmental acceptance of the energies that are driving us. Practicing in an MSA retreat is discovering the Mandala of Now, an eternal dance of energetic patterns, all displaying confusions, suffering, and pain, alongside and highlighting the brilliant sanity that is endlessly present.

The Five Buddha Family Mandala styles have both an enlightened wisdom aspect as well as a confused shadow aspect to them. The notion is that each of the five Buddha Families has a color, a direction, an element, a style, a primary emotion, a realm of existence, and a comprehensive display of physical, energetic, and mental manifestations that all fit together. Each family relates to one of the five Skandhas as well, which are subtle movements of mind we use to create a tangible sense of ego. When these movements of the mind are uncoupled from the Skandha process of forming ego, then the interconnected and enlightened capacities of that movement of mind are revealed.

The Five Buddha Families are named Buddha, Ratna, Padma, Karma, and Vajra. We call them families because they are familiar to us; they are like family. In Contemplative Psychology, the Five Buddha Family Mandala is at the center of exploration and essential to discovering the diamonds that are innate within each of us. The five colors are representative of each family, also representing a season, an element, and a direction. Depending on the lineage, the Vajra family and the Buddha family sometimes exchange the colors blue and white. The colors also represent the colors of the rainbow, and the rainbow is an illusory example of something that is visible but can't be found. A rainbow body in the Tibetan culture signifies a fully enlightened Buddha.

Karuna Training's Approach to Maitri Space Awareness

In Karuna Training, we present MSA through seven-day retreats in three distinct stages to support participants to attune to the practice of space awareness and to help them develop equanimity or nonjudgmental awareness toward all five families. The wisdom and confusion aspects of each of the five families are often fascinating. This fascination quickly morphs into a preoccupation of categorizing oneself and others in a game of "what is my style?" Diagnosing Buddha Families is fun, but not particularly the point of the practice. Thus, in Karuna Training, we begin by introducing the families' correlation to their elemental nature. Each of the five families has one of the five elements according to the Tibetan system: space, earth, fire, wind, and water.

Starting with the five families' elemental makeup helps us remain unbiased because, typically, we do not demonize the elements. As we study the elements, we realize they are the substantial makeup of all phenomena. For example, when it rains on our parade and our plans must change due to wet weather, we typically do not blame the rain as the object of our disappointment, unless we are thinking like a young child. The rain is primordially good; the rain is neutral and inconveniently collided with our plans. Boohoo! We don't need to reject or accept the rain or water altogether. The ability to suspend blame and judgment is essential in developing maitri for ourselves and all the energies and phenomena that make up the Five Buddha Families.

The next level of understanding the depth of the MSA mandala includes the emotional and psychological components of the five families. The study is one of the energetic inseparability of wisdom and confusion in one's body, speech, and mind, as well as the reflection of others' energy in the group, often so different than our own, letting us investigate the nature of mental conditioning and habitual styles. The correlation with the Five Buddha Families and the Five Skandhas, introduced in chapter III, is investigated in terms of the subtle movements of mind: first split, feeling, perception, formations, and consciousness. Participants delve into the five poisons: passion, aggression, ignorance, pride, and jealousy. And equally explore their correlate wisdoms: compassion, mirror-like wisdom, all-encompassing space, equanimity, and all-accomplishing action.

Maitri Space Awareness in Karuna Training ushers in teachings that emphasize *intensification* practice. This practice is also jokingly referred to as the "bloat and pop" method of *transmutation.* Chögyam Trungpa explains that transmutation means "the neurotic expression of any Buddha family can be transmuted into its wisdom or enlightened aspect."[22] Transmutation is a shift of awareness, revealing reality to be as it is, versus our version of what we think it should be. Contemplative Psychology utilizes the practice of Compassionate Exchange as a vehicle of transmutation in working with others. This topic will be covered extensively in future chapters. Thus, the MSA retreats are designed to successively bring participants into a deeper understanding of the play of energies as organized into the Five Buddha Family Mandala. MSA evolves one's trust and faith in intrinsic sanity to a deeply held experience of *brilliant sanity.* The diamonds within us are revealed and shine—becoming extremely beneficial in working with others.

A Fuller Understanding of the Five Buddha Families

As Chögyam Trungpa explains, The Five Buddha Families are an ancient delineation of "five aspects of the totality (of existence). We

---

22 Trungpa, Chögyam, "The Mandala of Unconditioned Energy, 'Ordinary Chaos'" in *The Collected Works of Chögyam Trungpa, Volume 6* (Boston & London, Shambhala 2004) pp. 358-359.

are talking about one aspect from five different angles."[23] And then there are the Five Buddha Families of each individual family. The teachings on these families include an element, a color, a dominant emotion, a confused emotional style, and an awakened wisdom manifestation. Most important to ego's mind map, the Five Buddha Families correlate with the Five Skandhas discussed in chapter II.

The association with the Skandha is important because we see that when that movement of mind is uncoupled from the ego's need to divide and confirm existence, then that same capacity of mind is a path to our intrinsic sanity and, ultimately, to our awakenment, or Buddhahood.

Beginning in the mandala's center, we start with the *Buddha* Buddha family; the Buddha element is space. The color is white, and the challenging emotion is ignorance. The wisdom of the Buddha family is *all-accommodating space,* which describes the natural openness that is our birthright. Buddha is associated with the first Skandha: "first split." "First split" is a nuanced and subtle occurrence of separating into duality, and it's very unconscious and hidden to most of us. However, when we're not divided in duality, then we're naturally resting in nonduality. Bringing awareness to nowness is how to discover the all-pervasive accommodation of space—a space whereby we innately synchronize with our intrinsic health.

Moving to the southern domain of the Five Buddha Family Mandala, we encounter the *Ratna* Buddha family; the element associated with Ratna is earth. The color is gold, and the challenging emotion is pride, which sometimes can be inflated arrogance or the other end of the spectrum—the poverty of not being, doing,

---

23 Trungpa, Chögyam, "The Mandala of Unconditioned Energy, 'Ordinary Chaos'" in *The Collected Works of Chögyam Trungpa, Volume 6* (Boston & London, Shambhala 2004) pp. 358-359.

or having enough. The wisdom of the Ratna family is *equanimity*, the ability to rest in nonjudgmental awareness without accepting or rejecting ourselves and the world around us. Ratna relates to the second Skandha: feeling. Feeling Skandha reinforces the first Skandha by energetically checking to ensure we feel safe; everything external is met with either safe, unsafe, or neutral. The feeling Skandha is a subliminal and primarily unconscious preverbal inquiry experienced on a gut level, energetically. However, if we can engage the capacity of mind that feels energetically, without the need to protect our ego, then we discover the experience of equanimity.

Moving clockwise through the mandala, we encounter the *Padma* Buddha family in the western domain; the Padma family element is fire. The color associated with Padma is red, and the challenging emotion is desire, specifically attachment. The wisdom of the Padma family is discriminating awareness, which is this interconnected knowing of what to accept and what to reject. The Skandha associated with the Padma family reinforces the first two Skandhas: perception/impulse. The mind's movement is engaged in accepting and rejecting or ignoring, due to feeling neutral. When the energy of the Padma family is uncoupled from the ego's need to fortify itself, a knowing awareness is engaged, which is called *Prajna*. Prajna is the kind of wisdom that sees through the solidity of ego's game and sees innate space. This interconnected knowing is how our basic sanity is both fostered and protected.

Moving to the north, we encounter the *Karma* Buddha family; the Karma family element is wind. Karma here means "action," as opposed to the usual understanding of cause and effect. The color associated with Karma is green, and the challenging emotion is either jealousy or envy. Both jealousy and envy work with a comparative mind; jealousy is protecting that which we believe is ours, and envy is coveting that which we desire and others possess. The wisdom is all-accomplishing action, as Karma here is translated as action versus the Sanskrit understanding of karma as cause and effect. The Skandha associated with Karma is formation, where we solidify duality with language, labels, and fixed mental formations. When we do not enlist this capacity of mind to formulate our existence habitually, we can utilize the comparative mind to its greatest advantage. For example, the ingenuity of humans to "build a better widget" comes from comparing one idea to another and advancing better conditions or solutions for the world. This active labeling mind is something unique to human beings, both fostering ingenuity and creativity as well as dangerously labeling and othering too.

Finally, we have a fully formulated mandala moving to the east with the *Vajra* Buddha family, the element of which is water. The color associated with Vajra is blue, and the primary conflicted emotion is anger. The Vajra family is the most solidified of the families, with the Skandha being full-blown consciousness. Vajra wisdom is mirror-like, which is the capacity to reflect all aspects of reality simultaneously. When the ego's Skandha mechanism does not co-opt this movement of mind, the unhooked impetus of the mind sees the multidimensional truths of phenomena extremely clear. The Vajra capacity of the mind to reflect on the interconnected whole is the capacity to hold the view of a fully enlightened Buddha and to evoke one's innate, intrinsic health that is imminently present in nowness.

How the MSA practice and the Five Buddha Family Mandala translates on the journey of Contemplative Psychology is through deepening and extending the tradition of mindfulness-awareness. Space awareness practice depends on a stable and clear mind, which has already been processed by meditation practice. MSA cultivates a more refined and nuanced relationship to space and is an extension and sophistication of mindfulness-awareness meditation.

Over time, we discover more and more subtle capacities of how we split off from our interconnected nondual relationship to space and from our intrinsic health. We do so through feelings, perception, habits of discernment, and an opinionated entrenched knowing, and the unique patterns of solidifying ego become more and more conscious to us. The awareness of these subtle movements of the mind is only available to us through the present moment of nowness.

Through MSA practice, the understanding dawns that *this* moment is the only moment we truly must wake up. This moment is the only portal we must touch into the illusion of our self-imposed separation or *duality*. To perceive *nonduality* requires a mind refined with nuanced awareness, a mind willing to experience the inseparability of "this and that," and a mind that has faith and experiential trust in basic sanity.

The mandala of now is ever-present and can be explored through the practice of MSA. The point of this elaborate awareness of space and form is to gain faith and confidence in our intrinsic health and, ultimately, the basic sanity of others and the world. Through the simple act of returning to now and raising our gaze, we experience, again and again, that we can evoke our innate basic health.

Synchronizing our body, speech, and mind in the present moment and attuning to space is our method. By doing so, we are habituating and even ritualizing the capacity to relax into the inseparability of confusion and wisdom. Nonduality occurs in tiny glimpses at first and cannot be the goal. It's more of a ripening of meditation practice in our minds, which takes time, patience, and perseverance. It's a process of genuinely befriending ourselves as we are.

Section Two

Taking Emotions as Path

CHAPTER VII

Building Intensity Capacity

We turn our attention now to owning our emotions so we can use emotional energy to wake up instead of acting out or going to sleep. Diving into a more nuanced embodied awareness of our emotions through contemplative methods develops our intensity capacity. Strengthening our capacity to remain present with emotional intensity is necessary to transmute emotional confusion into wisdom. Techniques such as the Four-Step Practice are discussed in this section to ritualize and embody "staying with" emotional energy as it arises, versus suppressing or acting out the energy in destructive ways. The practice of neither accepting nor rejecting our or others' emotional energy is synonymous with practicing equanimity.

In Contemplative Psychology, working with emotions is a precursor to the development of compassion. We must first befriend and accept our energetic natures before embracing and aspiring to liberate others' suffering. Compassion, from a Buddhist perspective, means we desire to relieve the suffering of others. Thus, tuning into the omnipresence of phenomena we call *exchange* understands that only 30% of our communication uses words. The other 70% is happening nonverbally and has far more significance on our experience. Exchange is the capacity to feel others' emotions directly and inseparably through direct contact in the present moment. According to Contemplative Psychology, exchange occurs all the time, whether we choose to be aware of it or not.

Taking emotions as a path allows us to explore how exchange taps into the potency of *bodhichitta*, a Sanskrit word meaning the "awakened heart." Bodhicitta is another of the diamonds within us; however, bodhicitta must be cultivated and awoken within us, unlike intrinsic health, which is innately present. Bodhicitta has two aspects, relative and absolute, which must be continually discerned to evoke basic sanity.

Skillfully working with emotions creates the conditions for us to offer ourselves benevolently to help others. The fruition of Contemplative Psychology is the practice of *Compassionate Exchange*, the ability to evoke the intrinsic sanity in others on the spot. Through rousing our intensity capacity, we can stay present with others' emotional intensity through our processed awakened heart, or bodhicitta. Growing our heart's potential progress with attention to four capacities of heart: maitri (loving-kindness), compassion, sympathetic joy, and equanimity. These themes are explored deeply in the next chapter, but we must begin with the basics of identifying emotions and taking them as a path.

Recognizing Emotional Energy

Building Intensity Capacity, this first chapter of section two, introduces Contemplative Psychology's fundamental approach to working with emotions and the importance of attuning to the subtlety of emotional energy. A refined awareness is required to recognize and distinguish emotional energy as it arises. We often split off from our emotional energy due to past experiences or traumas. Sometimes we dissociate when we manifest or encounter uncomfortable feelings, such as jealousy, disappointment, or lust. In this chapter, we study how emotions function as a sophisticated operating system that can be accessed through contemplative practice. Contemplatively accessing emotions supports refining our awareness of space or trusting in our natural openness.

"Why on earth would we want to get into all this mucky emotional stuff?" That is what a "thinking-type" of person might say to themselves. However, when thinking-type people discover this whole instrument within themselves waiting to be played and voiced, they find a whole new world. There are those of us who are more "feeling-types," so emotionally fine-tuned that whenever we enter a room and encounter emotional distress in another, we instantly feel it fully. Sometimes "feeling-types" become accustomed to thinking what others are feeling is our fault. So learning how to navigate the land mines of emotions is a tremendous benefit for both thinking and feeling-type people.

Contemplative Psychology is about becoming familiar with our interior landscape, an emotional sensing world, the depths of which many of us have not had the permission or inclination to explore. In Contemplative Psychology, we dedicate a lot of time to familiarizing ourselves with the inner landscape of emotional tendencies. What are the habits of mind that correlate with the play of emotions?

First, it's essential to understand that emotions are something, and we access them through feeling. Emotions are there for a reason, and we don't need to manage them away. They are the portal to everything we love and know about the world. We could see them as the color of the world. I've worked with people in Karuna Training who didn't think they had emotions at all. It has taken some students the entire two years of basic training, 11 programs, to acknowledge a feeling—much to others' frustration in the group. But there is nothing wrong with these folks who cannot feel—it's only an expression of their conditioning—and thinking-type students bring other attributes to the group.

I often compare our emotions to a sophisticated internal operating system, perhaps something like an automated smart heating and cooling system, which we recently installed in our house. When we first installed this "smart" device, I didn't even understand how to turn up and down the thermostat. Smart appliances come with instructions, yet many of us are not prone to reading operating instructions, and therefore we never really learn how to use them properly. When they break down, we blame the technology. The same can be said for our emotions; they're an operating system that many of us never learned to operate or glean their benefits. Thus, we are left feeling frustrated by emotions we don't know how to control.

Emotions are made of charged thoughts, and thoughts are made of space. Our feelings are invisible forces that often rule us unless we learn how to ride them through mindfulness-awareness. Take a moment to contemplate problematic emotional energies that are challenging for you in your ongoing experience. Emotional conditioning is different for each of us due to our cultural and familial backgrounds and influences. Thus, we all respond differently to states of excessive desire, anger, and blatant stupidity.

For example, we allow and embrace some emotions such as cussing at strangers under our breath as customary in some cultures and families, more than others. Cussing under our breath doesn't mean what it might mean in quiet families. Screaming or loud speaking carries more reactions and significance to some than others.

We all have emotions that are allowed; for example, some folks cry during sentimental TV commercials, and some folks can easily say, "I love you," and mean it when they say it. Others cannot feel or express any vulnerability or intimacy due to their conditioning. We can allow for conditioning and biases to influence emotional habits—this is inevitable—and we can regard what we discover as "just information." Becoming nonjudgmental toward all emotional energy and increasing our familiarity with our emotional tendencies and habits leads to an increased capacity to feel their energetic intensity.

When we become aware of preferred emotions and habits of avoidance, or bypassing energy, we learn to see it all as "just information." This means we don't have to justify it through psychologizing why we are the way we are or come up with elaborate theories. We can simply touch the energetic experience through feeling and come back to the present, like in meditation practice.

The Four-Step Practice introduced in this chapter trains us in staying with emotional energy instead of trying to think our way out of feelings. Thus, we develop an even-minded approach to whatever we're feeling and experiencing. Meeting our emotions with a nonjudgmental awareness is feeling the energy directly as it arises in the present moment. This approach is both a challenge and the opportunity to awaken the wisdom of emotions. Our ability to feel feelings and sensations without judging them as good, threatening, or indifferent is the mark of developing *equanimity.*

The Four-Step Practice is considered training wheels for *transmuting* confused emotions into their innate wisdom. Transmutation sounds exotic and something like the alchemy of turning lead into gold; however, the process has much more to do with the metaphor of composting, using our garbage to its most significant benefit by staying with and burning through emotional energy as it is arising. As Chögyam Trungpa explains, "The irritating qualities of emotions are transmuted once you experience them as they are. Transmutation does not mean that the energy quality of the emotions is eliminated; in fact, it is transformed into wisdom, which is very much needed."[24]

We use the Four-Step Practice in Karuna Training[25] to lean into and stay with difficult emotional energy skillfully. I like to call this practice the training wheels of transmutation. The method can be accomplished very quickly or slowly, but it's important to begin by working with emotional energy step by step. Or one can linger on one step for a longer time. The point is learning how to feel emotional energy instead of thinking about it or trying to figure it out. We are practicing staying with the energy until it naturally changes and dissolves. Remember all emotional energy is dynamic by nature, and its natural course is to dissolve, resolving itself into openness and loosening the intensity of the feelings along the way.

---

24 Trungpa, Chögyam, "Tantra" in "Cutting through Spiritual Materialism" from *The Collected Works of Chögyam Trungpa, Volume 3* (Boston & London; Shambhala, 2003) p. 179.

25 The Four Step Practice was first introduced into Karuna Training by faculty Paul Cashman and has been procured as a methodology in the Karuna toolbox.

The Four-Step Practice

1. **Identify:** Begin by coming into the present moment
    and feeling into the body. We first drop out of the head
    and into the sensations of our body. In doing so, we find
    the place in our bodies where the energy is pooling or
    coagulating, where we feel sensations, and we stay with
    that place.

2. **Hold without judgment:** Once we've identified an
    energetic place in one or more parts of our body, we stay
    with it with an attitude of loving-kindness, like we are
    holding a baby bird that has fallen from a nest. We hold
    the energy, and through feeling, become curious about its
    texture, shape, intensity, etc.

3. **Bring the energy to heart:** Once we have been curious
    about the energy, we join it and become it fully and
    completely. We embody the energy fully, without
    interpretation or hesitation.

4. **De-identify with the energy:** Energy by nature is
    dynamic, and it will naturally dissolve. Sometimes,
    depending on the intensity of the emotion, it can stay for
    a long time. However, eventually, if we feel long enough,
    it dissolves. We can also intentionally raise our gaze and
    come fully into the present moment and thus dissolve the
    energy in nowness.

Embracing Emotions

Taking emotional energy as a path requires strengthening our mindfulness-awareness practice. We develop a refined perception of the invisible forces of emotional energies. The ability to stay with uncomfortable sensations increases our *intensity capacity*. This world and the emotions it evokes can be very intense and uncomfortable. Being human is intense, often highly inconvenient, and if ever we want to act benevolently toward others, we're going to need intensity capacity to do so.

Working with emotions from the perspective of Contemplative Psychology increases our intensity capacity. Emotions are the source of our greatest wisdom but not unless we develop the capacity to directly feel emotional energy.

Most of us learn to manage our emotions as if they are employees or pets, as something separate from ourselves. Strong emotions arising at the wrong moment are a nuisance and can be embarrassing, especially if we're easily emotionally flooded. We have stored mythologies about which emotions are unacceptable and why they should never be experienced. Emotions easily derail us when we don't understand what they are and why we feel them. How to work with them skillfully is our challenge. Life is more difficult when we do not know how to ride emotional energy.

Emotions are not separate entities that invade our minds temporarily as something alien. However, our language conveys this notion. We are regarding our emotions as separate when we say things such as, "I wasn't myself the other day," or "I'm sorry I screamed at you," or "I don't know what came over me," or "That wasn't me." Typically, we split off from our emotional energy and distance ourselves from any responsibility for the energy.

Emotions arise in the first place because they are a way for us to meet our truths. Emotions feel the way they do because they have something to express, and they bring our attention to something that needs addressing. On the other hand, sometimes emotions are habitual and reactive, and then they're not helpful, but only act to fend off interaction or guilt. Still, emotions can also be interpreted as "bad" before we've given the energy any space to be experienced or expressed.

We habituate our reactions to certain emotions so that when discomfort arises in us, we rudely say to ourselves "something's wrong with me," or "I shouldn't be feeling sad, upset, or jealous," or whatever it is we've decided to manage and suppress. When we avoid discomfort this way, we bring judgment to the moment, and this judgment is like a thick coating that blocks our capacity to feel and listen to ourselves. The contemplative way to listen to ourselves is through feeling, sensing, and experiencing what energy is expressing itself in the present moment. This is very different from trying to figure out why we feel a certain way, attempting to justify our feelings, and/or managing the emotions away.

Feeling emotional energy as it's arising takes the contemplative discipline of mindfulness-awareness, opening to energy as we bring our awareness to the body, exploring whatever we meet nonjudgmentally in the present moment and feeling the texture of the emotion with loving curiosity. Approaching emotional energy with respect is an alternative to suppressing energy or acting it out. This practice of feeling takes strong mindfulness to even notice emotional energy for what it is.

For 11 years I commuted between Petaluma, California, and San Francisco for my work. On many days, the drive was one and a half hours one way, and often the drive could stretch to two hours, due to dense traffic on CA Highway 101. For most of these years, it was habitual for me to feel aggressive toward other drivers. I also developed serious back pain, which seemed to worsen the more I screamed at other drivers. One day, I finally realized I'd not opened to this aggressive energy in a contemplative way and that I was indulging my anger.

I spent time feeling and contemplating my aggression while I was driving, first in my body and then with curiosity, I contemplated what was really going on inside of me energetically. I often found myself crying and feeling vulnerable once I started addressing the energy contemplatively. I began to understand my feelings were more about being trapped and oppressed in my car. I then realized this was something I was sharing with everyone else on the road simultaneously. I realized I was blaming other drivers for my life choices and making myself miserable. I began to see this in other commuters' faces. To me, they looked desperate, and I realized I looked the same.

Once I found my commonality with other drivers, the emotions turned into pure heartbreak. I recognized that living in the Bay Area and holding a job in the city meant commuting. Through ongoing contemplative work, I embraced my emotional energy while commuting. I decided to practice loving-kindness while driving, being gentle and generous toward myself and other drivers while commuting. This translated into always letting other drivers in the lane first, yielding on the road, and not rushing even when I was late. Eventually, I befriended the other drivers as mutually suffering commuters and held theirs and my own frustration in mutual sympathy. This led to a much more pleasant commute, and more importantly, my contemplations developed the wherewithal to convince my boss I only needed to commute three times a week to the city.

It is usually easier to start working with emotions by studying the confusing aspect of our emotional energy, or the *klesha* aspect of emotions. Klesha in Sanskrit means nuisance or defilements, so kleshas are energetic states that are solidified emotional blocks, which become part of the ego's mechanism of survival. I'm referencing the fourth Skandha, the intellect, as mental formations that habituate in our mind and psyche. We tend to recycle energetic states of mind, which become easily accessible through conditioned biases and environmental influences.

Five basic *root kleshas* or primary emotional states solidify ego and are considered problematic: ignorance, passion, aggression, pride, and jealousy. We consider them primary hues of energy, as with colors that have a primary hue: white, red, blue, yellow, and green. There is also an elemental component to emotions: ignorance is associated with space (openness or spacing out), passion is associated with fire (burning or flickering), aggression with water (freezing or boiling), pride with the element earth (solid and pervasive), and jealousy or envy is associated with wind (one-pointed and propagating). All these categories correlate with the Five Buddha Families and are all part of discovering the mind map of ego.

Emotional energy is dynamic by nature, meaning nature is continually changing unless we dam it up by suppressing the energy. This stream of feeling consciousness can be tapped into, honored through feeling, investigated with kindness, and from which the truth of the present moment can be discerned. We come to respect emotional energy as the messenger it is. Emotions allow us to contact our truth, which is also dynamic and ever-changing. All emotions contain wisdom from a Contemplative Psychology perspective.

How to Work Skillfully with Emotions

In Contemplative Psychology, there are three approaches to working with kleshas, and we train in all three. Emotional energy is being approached contemplatively, addressed through feeling in the present moment, utilizing the mental processes of "thinking." The mind is the portal to working with emotions contemplatively, which means we're working with form and space. Form and space in this context are body and mind, which we synchronize on the breath in meditation. This is our laboratory for investigating how to work skillfully with kleshas.

First there is approaching our emotions as charged thoughts. Seeing emotions for what they are serves to cool the emotions and allows enough space to not be completely ruled by the energy. All Contemplative Psychology methods begin on the meditation cushion, learning to see thoughts for what they are—"thinking." Meditation practice cultivates enough space to see emotions as nothing more than thoughts.

Seeing our emotions as thoughts doesn't mean we suppress them, which many people, unfortunately, use meditation to do. John Wellwood named the act of using meditation practice to avoid our emotions as "spiritual bypassing." This avoidance is obviously not the point of meditation; however, the idea is to create enough space and stability of mind through meditation, especially when our kleshas are hot like they can be with feelings of passion or rage.

Once we have enough space and stability of mind through meditation practice, then we can approach emotional energy more directly with loving-kindness and inquiry. This is the second approach to working with emotions and requires remembering that all energy ultimately possesses intrinsic health. Feeling into our emotional energies we uncover their innate nature, unexpressed wisdom. This requires our willingness to feel the energy for what it is, without a narrative. With difficult emotions, staying with feelings is what builds intensity capacity.

The ability to feel our emotions without attaching story is a big ask. It takes a great deal of mind-muscle to pull oneself out of the heat and into the felt sense of the body. When we learn to drop out of the head and into the body as emotional sensations are arising, we're dropping into the present moment. Feeling into the body, locating where energy pools in us, and then befriending the energy, no matter what it feels like. Once we dare to locate and feel the emotional energy, we stay with it by placing the sensations in the *cradle of loving-kindness.*[26] We stay with the energy through feeling with a gentle inquiry. By doing so, we train ourselves to feel emotional energy fully.

The Four-Step Practice is a technique that trains us to stay with energy as it is arising, with kindness and curiosity. The reason to stay with emotional energy is that all emotional energy by nature is dynamic, not static. Emotional energy is impermanent like everything else, and when we bring mindful feeling to our bodies, the energy naturally changes, dissolves, or morphs into something else.

Feeling energy directly is radically different from suppressing energy, which normally makes us sick, and we eventually end up with an implosion or depression. Another alternative to staying with energy is getting emotionally wild, screaming, or acting it out. The "who

---

26 Trungpa, Chögyam, "How to Cultivate the Great Eastern Sun" from *Great Eastern Sun: The Wisdom of Shambhala* (Boston & London: Shambhala, 2011), pp. 110- 111.

cares what you think" approach to emotions is an energetic indulgence, so to speak. Acting out emotions adds fuel to the fire and serves to make emotional energy stronger and more unruly.

Meeting the energy exactly as it is arising, through feeling and anchoring our awareness in the body, is the second approach. This is the capacity to drop out of the narrative in our head and into the body in order to feel emotional expression through sensations. Once we're stable in staying with energy, then we can use the energy to become more selfless. We do so by leaning into the energy as we feel it and intensifying it, which is purely feeling the sensation as opposed to getting hysterical.

The third approach to working with emotions requires grounded mindfulness-awareness and the ability to discern energy in a nuanced, refined way. This requires we drop all expectations of attainment, any hopes of insight or wisdom, and we simply become the feeling fully and completely. Because energy is dynamic and innately insightful, when we truly intensify, we can touch on the phenomena of transmutation. Transmutation is really the point of working with the Five Buddha Families and Maitri Space Awareness discussed in chapter IV.

The ability to transmute emotional energy is equivalent to learning to burn through emotional energy with our strength of awareness. We literally feel ourselves to the root wisdom in the emotion. To work this way with emotions requires profound intensity capacity and a deep trust and conviction in intrinsic health. When practicing this way, we are transcending ego and not concerned with maintaining our sense of who we are whatsoever.

As Chögyam Trungpa says, "Transmutation takes place with the understanding of shunyata (emptiness or egolessness) and then the sudden discovery of energy. You realize that you no longer must abandon anything. You begin to see the underlying qualities of wisdom in your life situation, which means that there is a kind of leap. If you are highly involved in one emotion such as anger, then by having a sudden glimpse of openness, which is shunyata, you begin to see that you do not have to suppress your energy. You don't have to keep calm and suppress the energy of anger, but you can transform your aggression into dynamic energy. It is a question of how open you are, how much you are really willing to do it. If there is less fascination and satisfaction with the explosion and release of your energy, then there is more likelihood of transmuting it. Once we become involved with the fascination and satisfaction of energy, then we are unable to transmute it. You do not have to completely change yourself, but you can use part of your energy in an awakened state."[27]

A transmutation is an advanced approach to working with emotional energy and is built on the understanding that our egos are not as solid as we think. These three approaches to working with emotions are progressive steps in learning to work contemplatively with emotions. Learning to stay with emotions through feeling takes a strong mind and genuine trust in one's intrinsic sanity. Otherwise, it is like being asked to stand outside in a thunderstorm with an antenna raised. It feels as if we might be fried alive.

Speaking the Microscopic Truth

Listening and feeling our emotional energy directly takes mindful discipline. It takes a strong mind to cut our thinking mind and drop into the body and feel. It takes intensity capacity in order to stay with emotional energy as it is arising and feel it directly.

---

27 Trungpa, Chögyam, "'Tantra', Cutting Through Spiritual Materialism" in *The Collected World of Chögyam Trungpa, Volume 3* (Boston & London, Shambhala, 2003) p 173.

Finally, the most advanced step is learning to put words to our feelings, which is equivalent to finding our voice and expressing out loud how we are feeling. Voicing our emotions is difficult for some due to our conditioning around what is okay to say, what we think others expect from us.

Discerning the microscopic truth of emotional energy is the first step in learning how to express our emotions genuinely and truthfully. Speaking the microscopic truth is the ability to say the bare minimum and simplest truth of what we're feeling when we're feeling it, without justification or storyline. For example, "I feel cold and tired," "I feel angry and avoidant," "I feel touched and teary," etc. We do not have to add a "because" to our truth. We do not need a reason for why we feel the way we do. In fact, inventing a storyline for why we feel the way we do often works to split off or distance ourselves from the energy.

I learned early in my family that anger was uncouth, unladylike, and unbecoming. Early on, I habituated the habit of suppressing my anger, but that didn't stop me from feeling it or acting it out. Mostly I turned it on myself internally and made myself wrong for everything. Anger has a purpose; it is what allows us to say no when we need to do so. Obviously, there is a time to say no and there is a time to set boundaries; without anger and the clear-seeing that comes with it, we're not able to set appropriate boundaries for ourselves or others.

Through Contemplative Psychology, I learned to feel the *microscopic truth* of my energy, and especially discern when I'm feeling anger. Over time I've found my voice in expressing anger appropriately, and along the way, I swung to the opposite extreme of expressing anger too directly. When I found my voice, my anger could explode unreasonably, once I took the lid off. It has taken several years to learn how to discern the microscopic level of anger when it's arising so that I can be responsible for it. I now know when I'm getting angry; I feel the heat in the back of my neck and rushing energy in my head. A kind of electrical surge overcomes me, and when I catch the microscopic level of the energy, I can be with it in a way that allows me to investigate and contemplate. Again, we can never think our way out of anger, or any emotion for that matter; we need to start with a feeling.

In Karuna Training, my late colleague Gisela Von Keiser came up with the phrase and practice of "speaking the microscopic truth" as a discipline of first discerning, then labeling the minute glimmer of emotional energy as it's arising. She introduced the ritual of a group check-in using the microscopic truth of the present moment.

Speaking the microscopic truth is liberating because we begin to understand that what we say at this moment will certainly be different in the next. Speaking the microscopic truth is also generous toward others in that others don't want or need to hear why we feel the way we do unless they ask. Often our explanations around our feelings are simply too much information for the listener. The opportunity in hearing another's microscopic truth allows us to leave it alone; we learn to allow others their feelings and not feel responsible for them.

Becoming familiar with our personal habits of inhabiting emotions, which emotions we suppress, and which feelings we tend to act out, is an important piece of the journey of Contemplative Psychology. Ultimately, the task is making friends with ourselves by befriending and staying with our emotional tendencies. We become more intelligent in working with others and expressing our own feelings, and that's something for which the world is longing.

CHAPTER VIII

The Refined Heart of Awareness

As an early meditator I received a teaching that *your personal home environment reflects your habits of mind.* Once I got home that night and looked around my room, all I saw was chaos and clutter. I took this idea immediately to heart and cleared away tons of unnecessary clutter. The next morning, I began making my bed at age 24, for the first time in my life.

Forty years later, I still make my bed, hang up my clothes, and tidy up the spaces I'm occupying no matter where I am (except in hotels when there is service). Seeing the interconnectedness of mind and environment allows me agency to infuse my mind with tidiness in the present moment through my environment. Developing this discipline of cleaning up my personal space has been an act of kindness toward myself, and by now, it doesn't feel like a chore.

How we move through ordinary tasks in life directly affects our minds and our mood. The mind is infused with uplifted kindness simply by uplifting our environment. In Sanskrit, the word *citta* is the same word for both mind and heart, signifying that human beings have long understood these two aspects to be connected. We are now venturing into methods that serve to tame the mind and heart with *bodhicitta*, which means methods that awaken our mind and heart simultaneously. Bodhichitta is also the portal to tapping the wisdom faculty of the mind. Bodhicitta requires joining the head and heart, meaning marrying intelligence and warmth in all relationships to self and others.

This chapter dissects the Four Limitless Capacities of Heart: love, compassion, joy, and equanimity. To unlock the limitless capacity of heart, we train in Contemplative Psychology with the practice of *exchange*. The practice of working with exchange requires we presence ourselves, tune into what we are feeling, and utilize whatever energy we meet within ourselves as a resource to tune into the experience of other. Working with exchange is about developing the practice of oscillation, a purposeful awareness that oscillates between our inner and outer sensed experience. We tune in to the "felt-sense" of our immediate experience, both inside and outside ourselves, and then we do our best to welcome the emotional energy and to stay with it, as it is. Opening to discomfort becomes our path and proves to build potential of heart. The practice of working with exchange makes us brave.

The ancient practice of Tonglen meditation is a method that Buddhism has developed that requires this same mental oscillation anchored on the in- and out-breath. On the in-breath, taking in suffering, and on the out-breath, giving away the bottomless nature of bodhicitta. Tonglen is a method that grows the potency of heart by taking the grit of one's existence and shining the jewels of brilliant sanity. On the path of Contemplative Psychology, we mine for these diamonds within us and offer them as engaged compassion in the world.

Developing Maitri: Loving-Kindness

Again and again we return to the meditation cushion, befriending ourselves in unmitigated open space, which means meeting ourselves as we are, in the present moment. I've been practicing meditation for a long time, almost 40 years. As I've already confessed, my discipline with meditation didn't come easily, and meditation was not easy to integrate into my daily existence. In the first eight or so years, the practice experience didn't mean anything to me because I could not translate it into something useful. Thus, I struggled to wait by for the periods to be over or something to happen, like a lightbulb of insight or some proverbial "aha" to arise. Still, when I practiced, nothing happened until I finally relaxed with myself as I was. Meditation is a process of wearing out deep levels of anxiety and self-hatred to arrive home to me.

Honestly, if the information now available about trauma would have been available in the 1970s, I probably would have been instructed in meditation quite differently. We know a lot more about necessary access to mindfulness and the nervous system's capacity to synchronize body, breath, and mind in the present moment. I began on the meditation cushion with unconscious, yet severe, anxiety. In those early years, I was too dissociated from my body to discern any sitting meditation benefits.

If you do enough meditation, the practice refines one's awareness, which allows access to feeling the subtle shifts that occur in our body, speech, and mind. However, first, we tame our minds to be fully present. As we discussed in the last chapter, sitting with ourselves as we are requires intensity capacity. For some, that capacity is more complicated than for others, depending on past environmental conditioning.

In earlier chapters, we looked at the quality of maitri, or making friends with ourselves, softening to the ills of the world, and opening to others' presence with gentleness and kindness. Chögyam Trungpa talks about maitri in this way: "The key point in overcoming aggression is to develop natural trust in yourself and your environment, your world. In Buddhism, this trust in yourself is called maitri. Maitri can be cultivated in yourself and other people; you can cultivate kindness and warmth. When you express sadness to others, then they, in turn, begin to find natural warmth within themselves. So, the Buddhist approach to working with people—especially those who were raised in difficult environments—is to provide a gentle, accommodating environment for therapy and teaching."[28]

In meditation, we practice with an attitude of ultimate kindness and acceptance toward ourselves, no matter how we feel in the present moment. Making friends with ourselves means we naturally relax with ourselves, as we are. If we sit with genuine kindness toward ourselves enough, eventually, this friendly warmth naturally spills out and radiates to others. Meditation is a softening process, and it works much like a hair conditioner or fabric softener. We soak ourselves in silence and breath, and we begin to experience ourselves and others around us with more ease and fewer tangles. The direct experience of befriending ourselves is that we become more gentle and responsive human beings.

The Four Potencies of Heart

Maitri

Maitri is the first of Four Potencies of Heart, capacities cultivated through meditation and many other experiential methods in

---

28 Trungpa, Chögyam, "Creating Environments of Sanity" from *The Sanity We Are Born With: A Buddhist Approach to Psychology* (Boston & London: Shambhala, 2005) p. 146.

Contemplative Psychology. Traditionally, in Buddhism, these are called the Four Limitless Ones. Through the cultivation of these four portals of expansiveness, we're able to step beyond a limited idea of who we think we are and discover the unlimited potential of the human heart. Circumstances for which the capacities of the heart can be applied are endlessly available to us.

Maitri is limitless love, as opposed to grasping love. Maitri is the aspiration for happiness, both for us and others' happiness. It is pure and unconditional, like the love a parent feels instantly with a newborn baby at the moment of birth—a love that's untainted by attachment. We can contemplate where we experience such love in our lives. Many of us already have examples of such love, and it manifests in different ways for each of us. I've always cared for animals; dogs, cats, birds, rabbits, but mainly dogs have held this unconditional space of love in my life. Long before service animals were in vogue, I've known how animals access this unconditioned selfless place in me. My animals have gifted me back with unconditional love, and yet it's been a pervasive, stabilizing, energetic bond between us.

People who hate themselves are blocked from unconditionally loving another being. Self-hatred arrests the heart's capacity to care and be responsive to others genuinely. There is a path to opening our hearts to ourselves and others. Often, we don't have space or capacity to open because self-hatred blocks the heart like a dirty air filter blocks fresh air. The accumulated habits of condemning ourselves occupy us and serve to help us avoid vulnerability. We make friends with ourselves only through touching and feeling our vulnerability. Contemplative Psychology is a path to accepting our deficiencies. Contemplative methods, like meditation, support us to move closer to ourselves without judgment. Softening ourselves to ourselves is the antidote to self-hatred.

I lived in Europe for nine years, traveling and teaching Contemplative Psychology, and was blessed to see my American cultural habits reflected to me through the eyes of several Eastern, Central, and Western Europeans. The reflection was always the same: Americans are seen as somewhat superficial in relationships; with our positive, friendly ways, we believe ourselves to make friends easily. During my time in Germany, France, and Slovenia, where I lived, I found it challenging to make friends in the American way. A kind reflection someone once told me was, "In America, if you have dinner with someone or go out a few times you call yourself 'friends,' but in Europe, we understand that true friendship requires hardship, and you have to survive something together to call yourselves true friends." I deeply contemplated this feedback and realized how accurate this analogy applies to the accomplishment of maitri. Maitri means accepting all aspects of ourselves or another—the good, the bad, and the ugly!

Maitri is a necessary first step in the development of bodhicitta. Before we can genuinely aspire that others be free from suffering, we must first make friends with ourselves and others. We must be responsive and open first before we aspire to relieve their pain and suffering.

Compassion

Compassion, or *karuna* in Sanskrit, is the second limitless capacity of the heart. Compassion is the genuine desire to alleviate the suffering of others. With this unlimited capacity of heart, we leave concern for ourselves behind. We no longer are maintaining barriers of protection when we open fully to others' woes and suffering. This openness is where our trust in intrinsic health or basic sanity comes in as does our training in staying with emotions. In Contemplative Psychology, we strengthen our compassion by increasing our intensity capacity to open to and stay with others' pain.

Compassion is a word grossly misunderstood in our modern world; mostly we confuse compassion with notions of sympathy and empathy. Sympathy is arousing pity and sorrow for someone else's misfortune, which can imply a subliminal hierarchy with ourselves in the more favorable position. Empathy is the ability to share the feelings of another, from a place of identifying and understanding, but still being a fully separate and intact person. However, in Contemplative Psychology, the limitless capacity of compassion occurs in a relationship of equals. Compassion from a Contemplative Psychology perspective focuses on there being no hierarchy of the haves and have nots and no separation between us and another. The depth of our boundless compassion means we fully identify inseparably with another's pain and are willing to exchange our well-being with the other's suffering, thus touching into the nonduality of compassion.

Ideas like self-compassion so prevalent in today's "mindfulness parlance" are another way that compassion is misunderstood. Self-compassion serves to bring back the notion of wanting to relieve the suffering of ourselves, but in Contemplative Psychology, self-compassion is a bit of a misnomer. This sense of caring for ourselves is a form of maitri rather than compassion. There are no problems with the desire to relive our suffering, but the antidote is making friends with ourselves as we are. The term self-compassion misses an essential aspect of compassion itself—the sense of selfless boundaryless connection between self and others.

From a Buddhist perspective, the role of selflessness, known as *emptiness*, has a distinct function in developing genuine compassion. True compassion is said to be *as rare as a star in the daytime*[29]

---

29 Patrul Rinpoche, The Words of My Perfect Teacher (Boston: Shambhala: 1998)

because one must be entirely beyond ego for genuine compassion to occur. Most of us can experience compassion in micro-moments of experience but understanding the development of compassion is an intentional path of discovery. That's why so much attention is given to maitri first as a necessary step in rousing the heart's potency. Francesca Fremantle describes it this way: "Compassion is not just a feeling of pity or empathy, but an active force, the fundamental energy that is ceaselessly at work to remove the causes of suffering. It cannot help arising, because, in the realization of emptiness, there are no boundaries between self and other. Compassion is absolute sensitivity, unbiased love, and limitless concern for everything in existence. It is the natural outward expression of the bliss of enlightenment." [30]

When we encounter an unhoused person on the streets, for example, and offer them money, we must look at our motivation at that moment. Do we make eye contact? Do we fear they will use the money we offer to harm themselves? Do we feel embarrassed that we have so much and they so little? In this common scenario, all these responses are naturally sympathetic thoughts that arise from the heart's potency, but not necessarily genuine compassion. Most of us generously offer the homeless money from a space of sympathy or charity and not genuine compassion. To provide homeless people money from genuine compassion would mean, in the moment of offering, we feel our own homelessness fully and completely. Thus, genuine compassion occurs in a relationship of equals without a hierarchy.

---

30 Fremantle, Francesca, "Liberation: Uncoiling in Space" from *Luminous Emptiness: Understanding the Tibetan Book of the Dead* (Boston & London: Shambhala, 2001), p. 39.

Sympathetic Joy

Similarities further dissolve our tendencies of egoic preservation with the third limitless one, sympathetic joy. This capacity of the heart transcends our comparative mind and allows us to experience selfless joy, a joy that is genuinely delighted with the success of another. We are all conditioned to compare ourselves to others and establish in our mind's eye a hierarchy of who is on top and who is the lowest in society. Depending on our conditioning, we can use a symphony of topics to compare ourselves to others: beauty, age, wealth, class, skin color, degrees, accomplishments, talent, awards, someone else's attention, reputation, etc. Our modern economies are driven by our comparative human instincts, which are at the heart of much self-abuse, one-upmanship with others, blind privilege, and primitive beliefs about self-preservation and survival.

However, sympathetic joy is the cultivated capacity to celebrate another's accomplishments, talents, and success. We are, again, left out of the equation and unconditionally happy for the achievements and success of others. Sympathetic joy is like being a grandparent to the entire world; we celebrate others' happiness and wins like they are all our grandchildren. We are not congratulating ourselves for our accomplishments in others; we experience pure joy for others, without attachment to our contributions or support of the success. Sympathetic joy is pure joy!

Equanimity

Finally, through these progressive steps of cultivating the limitless capacities of the heart, we master the ability to meet everything wholly and directly in nonjudgmental awareness, which is equanimity. Equanimity is the fourth limitless capacity of the heart. We are harking back to Chapters II and III, where we talk a lot about developing "nonjudgmental awareness," what we call the stepping-stone to the development of the limitless capacity of equanimity.

Equanimity is a further development beyond nonjudgmental awareness. The ability to notice, stay conscious with, be kind toward, be open to, and let go of our mind's reactions is an embodiment of equanimity. Equanimity is a peaceful open approach to meeting the constant challenges of life. Evoking equanimity is remembering that openness is our natural state. Remembering that we get caught in mental formations and developing humor is an excellent way to soften reactiveness.

The ability to pull ourselves mentally present, out of fixated mental states and judgments, is a method that induces personal peace within us, and this radiates to others. We are all relieved in the business meeting or the family discussion when someone in the group can level and calm everyone down who is upset. This ability to alleviate upheaval is the potency and radiance of equanimity, its embodied basic sanity.

One Karuna student named the fruit of equanimity as *gaining more internal real-estate*, which is space to feel into those scary moments when we feel a contraction. To find this equanimity, we evoke the stability and balance of mind by not accepting or rejecting our experience. All experience is "just information," and that's that. Equanimity grows our bodhicitta because it grows acceptance and generosity within us.

Equanimity is the product of a processed heart, one that has been tested and strengthened with the grit of our foibles. We gain the ability to hold our own or another's experience in the space of complete equality. When we view our experience with equality, we find balance in the natural paradoxes of life. How we hate and love abides together within us, how competition and admiration coexist, how sorrow and happiness are often a resounding note in our hearts and play on in the continuum of our lives.

Exchanging Self with Others

Exchange is a word we work with a lot in Contemplative Psychology. It is defined as the natural and choiceless capacity to feel another person's feelings when in their vicinity. Exchange is not limited to people; we can also exchange with environments, like how haunted houses make us feel scared, or exchange with desire the way all commercials are designed to make us think. We navigate our lives with the capacity of exchange, yet mostly we're reacting to exchange in a way that creates further barriers between ourselves and the world.

When we first encounter someone in the morning, for example, whether they are our familiar partners at home, a coworker, or the person selling us coffee at Starbucks, we can experience energetic output in the form of "vibes" from another person. In Contemplative Psychology, we call those lively vibes exchange.

Usually, we feel something negative about another person, and we think things about the person we've made up in our minds! We say to ourselves, "They're in a bad mood today." When people are very familiar, we are likely to think something very habitual like, "They don't like me," or "They are mad at me," or "I did something wrong." The project of making things up is called *projection*. Exchange is the primary material we use to make projections, which are beliefs or ideas that we've made up about another person when we have not checked out if we are correct. Our projections might be accurate reads on the energy with which we've exchanged. However, they are also fabricated and don't allow for nuanced reasons for another person's energy. False projections drive entire relationships through the process of an inaccurately interpreted exchange, and once opened to, people find out how wrong they were in interpreting a silent exchange.

I had a distant acquaintance in my spiritual community for over 40 years, and I had encountered her the first time when we were very young. I had interpreted an exchange we'd had one evening around a mutual attraction. We didn't speak at the time, but I made up that she hated me and distrusted me as a person. Thus, I avoided her for many years and only interacted cordially and superficially when we met. One evening we found ourselves sitting together at a party with a glass of wine, and I was open enough to ask her how she felt about the age-old incident and her feelings about me all these years. I shared my projection with her and owned it as such. She laughed out loud and said, all these years, I thought that it was you who hated and distrusted me and thought I was distasteful. She then said she had always admired me but never felt there was an invitation to speak.

Misinterpreting exchange is a ubiquitous and ordinary thing we do with our acquaintances all the time. Then we decide on a hierarchy of whether people matter enough to address it. Exchange is happening whether we are conscious of it or not. As in the second and third Skandhas, discussed in "Chapter II: Ego Is Not the Enemy," we see that we are navigating our lives through the process of exchange. In the second Skandha called feeling, we use exchange to perceive if we feel safe, unsafe, or neutral. Exchange is a preverbal thermometer on whether we are in hostile territory. In the third Skandha, called perception impulse, we are discerning like, dislike, or couldn't care less, which impacts the relationship's nature. To be able to exchange with the space for safety and determine what to do and how to react is part of our basic sanity, and exchange is also a source of tremendous confusion and misinterpretation about others.

In Contemplative Psychology, we cultivate our faculty of exchange by exercising together with others in contemplatively experiential work. Learning to identify exchange while it is occurring and, with maitri, investigating how we are experiencing another's energy sheds a lot of insight into our habits of mind. For example, we can learn to ask, "How are you doing?" instead of making assumptions when someone is feeling bad (especially making the upset be about us when it often is not). We can learn to feel another's energy as "just information," thus increasing our equanimity toward all energies and circumstances we encounter in life.

In Compassionate Exchange, we learn to offer ourselves through the potency of heart to another and exchange self with another in nondual exchange. We will explore this in much more depth in the next two chapters; however, exchange is the medium by which we train in Contemplative Psychology.

Taking and Sending; Refining Our Heart Awareness

There is an ancient practice from Tibetan Buddhism called Tonglen; "Tong" in Tibetan means sending, and "Len" means taking, as in taking on another burden. Tonglen is the meditation practice that uses the medium of the breath to cultivate the heart's potency. We visualize taking on the pain and suffering of another by breathing in on the in-breath, and then exchanging our good fortune, privilege, sanity, and well-being with another by breathing that out toward the person on the out-breath.

Tonglen is an extension of sitting meditation, a development of meditation utilizing the breath to cultivate selflessness and open to the human heart's potential. Usually, we are warding off pain and danger outside and holding close to that which we cherish. The practice of Tonglen reverses this tendency and is a preliminary attempt to exercise the heart's four potencies. We breathe in the suffering of another on the in-breath and breathe out whatever would relieve another; that is the reverse of our ego tendency, so with Tonglen we exercise the openness of heart, like a muscle we work at the gym, only this time we are using our mind.

I must confess that after receiving formal Tonglen instruction, it took me around seven years to be able to practice for an entire 10-minute session of Tonglen. Most of the time, I dissociated at the mention of Tonglen and returned when the timekeeper rang the gong telling us the Tonglen session was over. That was information that my mind was not tame enough to train the openness of the heart.

When I found myself in the throes of therapeutic practice many years later, leading up to five hours of process groups in a women's in-patient hospital, only then I discovered the value of Tonglen. My friend and fellow Karuna teacher, Terry Jaworski, coined the term *Guerilla Tonglen* for when we utilize Tonglen in the presence of another, silently with or without them knowing. I often found myself on the precipice of panic in these difficult-to-manage process groups and found when I resorted to Guerilla Tonglen on the spot, breathing in the group's collective pain and breathing out essential health and brilliant sanity, almost always something would move.

While Tonglen is very practical for the practitioner, it's undetermined whether it measurably contributes to others. Either way, Tonglen helps us to grow a refined potential of heart.

Tonglen Instructions

Again, I am offering you practice instruction that would be easier to receive in person; however, I will provide the classic Tonglen instructions for those who may not have access to trained meditation instructors. Formal Tonglen is always practiced in the context of mindfulness-awareness practice so that we are arising with a stable, open, and settled mind before beginning the taking and sending method.

1. First, we flash on the open space of intrinsic health—the absolute open, unfettered awareness and unbound nature within us are aroused in a flash, something we rouse in ourselves, complete unconditional openness of bodhicitta.

2. The next step is to attune to the in- and out-breath, breathing in hot, claustrophobic, and heavy energy but without content, and on the out-breath, we breathe out light, open, kind, and spacious lifeforce. In a sense, we are warming up and synchronizing to the rhythm of taking and sending before attuning to the pain and content of our lives. This part can go for two or three breaths up to a few minutes. Sometimes we can't feel any synchronization and we must skip some breaths; all this is fine. Remember, Tonglen is a practice, and there is a path, like everything else, to Tonglen.

3.   Once we feel synchronized and in rhythm with breathing, even if we are skipping some breaths, the next step is to attune to content in our lives. Everyone knows of someone or a group of people who are suffering. Unfortunately, examples of suffering are bottomless in our world, and sometimes Tonglen is the only way we can integrate the pain of the world's grief. Here, we breathe in the suffering of another in the breath, imagining and feeling the pain, opening our hearts, and taking it on. Then we breathe out to that same person, relief from their suffering, happiness, and stability or ease. We imagine exchanging with their pain by taking it on and giving away all the good we have to offer them.

Note: Sometimes, we cannot coordinate and can't feel our hearts or find anyone or topic to open to; we don't have it in us. At that moment, we can use Tonglen to practice maitri with ourselves. We breathe in our own stuck, closed, blocked feelings and breathe out self-acceptance, love, and kindness. We may spend the entire session on this.

4.   A Tonglen session can go for three to 20 minutes.

5.   The last step is about growing our hearts even more significantly, and we consider the personal suffering we have been breathing in and know that there are thousands of others in our world experiencing the same pain. So we spend some time expanding our capacity to breathe in the suffering of others going through the same travails and breathing out to all of them the relief from suffering. This last step acts to expand the heart's capacity into further selflessness, love, and compassion.

6. Finally, to end the session, it is advised that we return to the primary practice of cultivating space within ourselves with mindfulness-awareness practice.

CHAPTER IX

A Mutual Path of Benevolence

Homing pigeons were once used as messengers in dangerous times, especially times of wars when villages were under siege, and there were no other means of communication. These pigeons always returned to their nests using something called magnetoreception, "a sense which allows an organism to detect a magnetic field to perceive direction, altitude, or location."[31] Magnetoreception is how the homing pigeons find their way home.

When we experience difficult emotions in another person, place, or object, we have a subliminal homing device through exchange within us, bringing awareness in communicating with others. This homing device acts through subliminal feelings, energetic sensations, and/or strong emotions. Most people unconsciously use an exchange as a subliminal warning system, especially if we're someone who avoids emotional intensity. We sense something going on in others, and we don't go there; we resist the impulse to pry more. We use this sensitivity to avoid issues, engage in superficial chatter instead, or become an artist at changing the subject.

---

31 Wiltshchko, Roswitha and Wiltshchko, Wolfgang, "Magnetoreception in Birds," *Journal of the Royal Society Interface*, September 2019; Volume 16, p. 58.

My late and vibrant father was like this, which is interesting because he surrounded himself with highly emotional women, beginning with his mother, my grandmother. During my teens and even younger, I made up that my father was incapable of emotions. Now, I think he was highly sensitive and felt everything, and he was a master at avoiding the messiness of emotions. He kept to himself with his homing device, exchange. I believe volatile emotions made my father feel ineffective, and he was all about getting the job done. When we don't know how the emotional operating system works, we tend to shut it down, stay close to home in our nests. Avoiding emotions can leave others feeling bereft and emotionally unmet.

Contemplative training utilizes the phenomena of exchange to deeply listen to our innermost sensitive cues; officially, these internal perceptions are called *interception*.[32] While the exchange is a choice-less capacity, we also use the word *exchange* to describe when we share these perceptions with another person. Learning to relate to internal sensations and impulses and then reflecting them openly to others is how we *offer an exchange*. What we typically do when we feel those subliminal feelings is we make things up out of our conditions. We sense someone is having a hard time and we make it about us; we think, "They don't like me," or "They are mad at me," or "They are impossible to deal with; there they are brooding again." Whatever we've projected onto people gets reinforced through the exchange.

Contemplative Psychology is a path of retraining ourselves to not make things up in our minds, but to rest in not knowing and learn

---

32 Interception is the perception of sensations from inside the body and includes the perception of physical sensations related to internal organ function such as heartbeat, respiration, satiety, as well as the autonomic nervous system activity related to emotions (Vaitl, 1996; Cameron, 2001; Craig, 2002).

to tolerate the intensity of the discomfort. We train to go toward emotional energy and open to it for the wisdom that is innate within the messiness of the feelings. Moving toward emotions is counter-intuitive to us without training. Also, most of us are unconscious around how we ignore and avoid feelings because much of this conditioning began to form in us when we were preverbal toddlers. Our environment conditioned us to hide and cower, or it encouraged us to show up and be adorable, to seek attention. Whatever the conditioning we bring, we all tend to have blind spots.

Exchange is the natural and choiceless capacity to feel another person's feelings in the present moment whether we are conscious of it happening or not. Working with exchange is enhanced through contemplative training and navigating the treacherous terrain of our difficult emotions. Along the way, we befriend ourselves and become skillful, compassionate friends for others. Contemplative Psychology presents a mutual path of benevolence.

In this chapter, we're treading the traditional ground of the Mahayana path of Buddhism.[33] Here, we learn to notice the micro-moments of experiencing unconditional open heart and investigate the steps to fully realize the ultimate bodhicitta, or awakened heart. These altruistic measures always start by examining our motivation, deciphering reality, and specifically examining how we discern the truth. On the path of Contemplative Psychology, we aspire to rouse our

---

33 Mahayana Buddhism refers to the Greater (Maha) Turning or Vehicle (Yana) of the Buddha's teaching. When the Heart Sutra was traditionally introduced, the explanation of "form is emptiness, emptiness also is form" was expanded on by Sariputra. The Mahayana is now practiced in a variety of forms of Buddhism in China, Tibet, Japan, and Korea. The tradition emerged around the 1st century AD. The path is concerned with altruistically oriented spiritual methods and is embodied in the ideal of the Bodhisattva.

bodhicitta and do so by using the grit of our human existence to shine the jewels of our awakened heart.

Contemplative Psychology invites the traditional Mahayana Buddhist teachings into our palpable lived experience. The methods of Contemplative Psychology curate micro-moments of openness that we learn to integrate into our body, speech, and mind. We cannot take the micro-moments of experiencing our interconnectedness for granted—the way a child smiles while sitting in the grocery cart, facing a long line at the check-out and their smile melts all impatience, the way you look up from your overwhelming desk to glimpse a crisp, bright February morning laden with wet snow and the promise of spring, the way your partner is trying to reason with you, and in doing so shares their utter heartbreak and pain. For a nanosecond, you glimpse the pain in their eyes and soften. You fully feel their pain and frustration, and their heartbreak becomes your heartbreak.

In Contemplative Psychology, we apply these teachings to our everyday interactions with others, the environment, and the world. Contemplative Psychology is a relational or a "communal" path of awakening; we name it a path of *mutual recovery*. Mutual recovery means there is no time off; this contemplative approach works on us 24/7 through our interactions in all our relationships with others. We begin to realize there's no relationship in our lives that's not worthy of love, respect, and openness. The quality of our relationships mirrors our minds and supports us to discover the diamonds within us.

Offering Exchanges Out Loud

Learning to express emotions out loud and still feel our dignity can take selfless courage. We all have developed habits of suppressing certain emotions and have well-established patterns in doing so. These coping mechanisms were intelligent to the circumstances at that time. Somewhere along the line, there were messages that certain feelings were not okay; perhaps that was anger or even love. The effect of that conditioning is that we no longer know what we feel.

I remember being smacked directly and hard across the mouth as a child for talking back. I don't even remember who hit me—a large, strong adult. I must have been about four, and there was a giant *no* in the space. It silenced my anger for decades, but I still felt the anger inside and turned it in on myself. In my family, this was appropriate discipline; I was not abused. Nevertheless, it conditioned me to watch my tone with authority.

In Karuna Training, we practice expressing our emotional states with others through mini-reflections, or what we call "offering an exchange." Training our capacity to offer an exchange occurs when we learn to say the microscopic truth, discussed in chapter V. We sense into the present moment and attune to an energetic feeling within us. Then we name it for ourselves and others, without explanations or justifications for the way we feel. "I feel shaky," or "I feel sad and sinking," or "I feel fresh and curious." All these microscopic truths stand on their own and don't need explanations.

The microscopic truth allows us to touch on what is happening in the present moment and honor our emotions with kind awareness. When hearing others' microscopic truths, we don't have to ask why all the time; we can allow people the space to have their feelings without needing to change or save them. Emotions are fleeting and brief when we don't tell a story to fortify them. In Contemplative Psychology, we soon learn we don't need to solidify our every momentary feeling as a solid belief. The practice of offering an exchange honors the dynamic nature of emotions and allows us the freedom to feel differently the next microsecond of experience.

The result of training in offering exchange and learning how to speak the microscopic truth allows us to express ourselves with fluidity and honesty in the dialog. Exchange is a navigational tool to both follow another's experience deeply and, along the way, reflect on what we're hearing. By attuning to others through offering an exchange, we develop a deep listening skill that integrates us through open-hearted compassionate listening.

Think about how it feels when we're in emotional turmoil and a good friend asks us about what is going on. Often that same friend will experience our discomfort and may try to talk us out of our feelings. People express their discomfort with emotions by saying things like, "It's not that bad," or "Things could be worse," or even offer us what can feel like superficial advice with sentences starting with, "You should do this or that . . .," etc. These conversations leave us feeling bewildered and not met.

In conversation, we desire to be acknowledged and listened to deeply, seen openly without platitudes of advice-giving or attempts at fixing us for feeling bad. Listening to a friend who is in emotional turmoil doesn't mean they need to be fixed unless they specifically solicit our advice for some reason due to true expertise. Emotional turmoil deserves a sympathetic ear with a gentle, nonintrusive reflection back, without someone trying to change us or talk us out of what we feel.

In Contemplative Psychology, we understand that the baseline of all emotions is intrinsic health, and even though there is often suffering involved, there is never ultimately anything to fix. And if there is something to change, then it's not the listener's work to do; it's the work of the person who needs to change. Sharing how the information lands for us in our bodies, emotions, and minds is received as a gift to others as a microscopic truth. The most compassionate way to listen to another person is through the thermometer of exchange.

We can also get overly absorbed in others' emotions, losing our bearing and feeling swallowed in an exchange. To not get lost in exchange, we use a practice called *oscillation*. Oscillating between self and other is touching into the other's experience fully and completely and letting go to come back home to ourselves. Our bodies in the present moment are our home base, and we land there to take the temperature of our exchange. If appropriate, we offer a reflection of what we find to the other through speaking the microscopic truth. Oscillating back and forth, we maintain equanimity in being available to another's emotions and are responsible for tracking how another's feelings are landing within us.

Working continually with exchange and oscillating back and forth between self and others is a responsive way to listen to someone who's in emotional turmoil. Like a homing pigeon, we are also kind to ourselves. We return again and again home to our bodies to temper the microscopic truth again and again. In Contemplative Psychology, the method of listening through exchange cultivates equanimity, or nonjudgmental awareness.

Aspiring and Entering

Chögyam Trungpa once said, "The basic vision of the Mahayana altogether is to allow people to think bigger, think greater. We can afford to open ourselves and join the rest of the world with a sense of generosity, tremendous goodness, and tremendous richness . . . the more we give, the more we are inspired to give constantly . . ."[34]

The practice of offering ourselves beyond ego means we're tapping into the treasury of nondual compassion. In nondual compassion, everyone is mutually liberated because there is no separation between self and others. In Contemplative Psychology, offering ourselves to others, compassionate exchange, is explored more deeply in chapter X. However, all the preparation is in learning to utilize exchange, and this starts by examining our motivation to be of benefit to others.

Awakening our bodhichitta is the outcome of practicing Compassionate Exchange. Along the way, it is essential to distinguish the two types of bodhichitta, often called two-fold bodhichitta. Two-fold bodhicitta articulates the progressive nature of developing compassion: first, a path of aspiring to benefit others (relative bodhicitta), and then a path entering the direct experience of being beneficial (ultimate bodhicitta), which we only glimpse in micro-moments of expertise.

We aspire to be of real benefit to others, and that opens the door to exploring the relative ups and downs of how the heart opens fully. Rock meets bone in our everyday life, and it's only in our everyday interactions that we can see our true motivation. True to Buddha dharma, the path of opening our hearts is fraught with embarrassing moments of seeing the strands of our selfishness, our ulterior motives, and all our blind spots.

I fluctuated wildly during a 12-year stint working as a therapist treating eating disorders and fighting the whole time with myself

---

34 Trungpa, Chögyam, "The Main Practice Which is Training Bodhichitta" from *Training the Mind and Cultivating Loving-Kindness* (Boston & London: Shambhala, 1993), p. 12.

around my true motivation. I had recovered from an eating disorder myself, or was in recovery like my clients, and today I must own that I still have imbalances with food. It is hard to be sane with food in our consumer, body dysmorphic society.

However, the real issues with my motivation were being challenged by the whole paradigm of psychotherapy. I was deeply questioning the way women have been diagnosed and pathologized in psychiatry from the onset. I found myself enraged at the psychological paradigm altogether and overly identified with the pain of the women I was treating. My righteousness around this became my motivation, proving the system wrong and talking my clients into their health in the face of real pathology. It became an obscuration and blighted the actual benefit of the therapeutic work. At some point, I knew I needed to distance myself from both being a therapist and treating women with eating disorders because my motivation or aspiration was too complicated.

First, there is the aspiration to be of benefit, and the beneficial behavior or service arises out of that pure motivation—"I want to be of help." Pure motivation is not "I want to be right," or "I want to be famous, and so I'm going to be helpful," or "I want to make a lot of money so I think I will be a doctor." Aspirations with a self-centered approach create suffering for all. We must ask ourselves when in the helping profession, what is our motivation if we truly wish to be beneficial?

The four limitless ones, maitri, compassion, joy, and equanimity, arise from a relative aspiration. In finding our limitless nature, we are working against ego's self-protection tendencies, and we're growing our potency of heart. Living openly and generously takes a great deal of discipline. It is not the kind of discipline involved in doing the right things or being a good girl or boy, but more an effortless discipline that arises from the pure motivation to be genuinely helpful and a desire to stop causing ourselves and others trouble and pain. Unfortunately, we can't get rid of the pain; we learn to feel it fully, befriend it, and ultimately transcend the pain into a path of humble benevolence.

Absolute and relative bodhicitta work together to awaken the potency of the heart. Francesca Freemantle describes this development: "At first, as relative bodhicitta, is the aspiration toward enlightenment for oneself and all beings; finally, as the ultimate bodhicitta, it is the state of wakefulness itself, the awakened heart and mind . . . It is the condition of being awake; Buddhaness, awakeness, wakefulness. It cannot belong to anyone; it is not yours or mine, even though we do sometimes speak of it loosely in that way."[35]

In Contemplative Psychology, glimpses of this wakeful bodhicitta, the heart's unconditional potency, arise when we surrender to things as they are in unbound openness. For example, experiences like a loved one's death are a hit of reality with which we cannot negotiate. When we surrender to the truth of death, we experience the relative pain and the absolute, unconditioned nature of impermanence. These experiences pierce us. That is the experience of ultimate bodhicitta; we are no longer there in the sense of egoic compromises. From a Contemplative Psychology perspective, the ultimate bodhicitta arises from opening to the world as it is complete. The world as it is is empty of ego and experienced as piercing reality.

---

35 Fremantle, Francesca, "Liberation: Uncoiling in Space" from *Luminous Emptiness: Understanding the Tibetan Book of the Dead* (Boston & London: Shambhala, 2001), p. 35.

In this unbound openness, nothing is fabricated. Usually, we only get small glimpses of ultimate bodhicitta. Through micro-moments or flashes of total selfless awareness, we open our hearts fully and completely. We are touched by the world and naturally responsive because we're not protecting ourselves; there is nothing to protect.

The work of developing our bodhicitta is much like the actual development of a pearl, as psychologist James Hillman reflects: "The pearl starts off as a bit of grit, a neurotic symptom or a complaint, a bothersome irritant in one's secret inside flesh, which no defensive shell can protect oneself from. This is coated over, worked at a day in and day out, until the grit one day is a pearl; yet it still must be fished up from the depths and pried loose. Then when the grit is redeemed, it is worn. It must be worn on the warm skin to keep its luster: the redeemed complex which once caused suffering is exposed to public view as a virtue."[36]

It is the grit of our lives, the irritants and all the unidentifiable emotional stuff that gets under our skin that serves to motivate us on a path of benevolence. In Contemplative Psychology, we process our unwanted and painful emotions in a way that produces potency, humbleness, and vulnerability of the heart. We use our life challenges, self-created or otherwise, to awaken the luster of our hearts, and it motivates us to offer ourselves to others selflessly.

Relative and Absolute Truths

Contemplative Psychology discerns between relative and absolute truths as a vitally important insight on the path to cultivating our

---

36 Hillman, James, *Insearch: Psychology and Religion* (Connecticut: Putnam, 1967), p. 56.

innate compassion. Understanding there is a distinction in our perspective of "the truth" is critical for working skillfully with others. It's often said that relative truth is what appears and absolute truth is how things are. We mostly see the world from a relative perspective; we know what we like and don't like and have justified these opinions in our minds somewhere along the line, which is a relative perspective.

At the heart of the Mahayana Buddhist path, the ultimate truth is pointed to—our natural unconditioned openness, our intrinsic health, and the innate potential of living with an awakened heart. Then we realize our relative perspective on life, believing everything that we think and our perspective on reality are not as solid as we thought. The ultimate dimension of truth understands the big truth that appearances are not as reliable as they appear to be.

The Buddhist cosmological view on the nature of *shunyata* (emptiness) becomes relevant in discerning absolute and relative truth. As you'll recall, shunyata is tapping into the unbound liberated nature of reality, which is utterly vast and open. Shunyata refers to everything being devoid of intrinsic nature, meaning nothing exists on its own.

Everything is interdependent. For example, your favorite wood stool in the garage is the product of a tree. It involved the craftsperson of the stool, the craft person's ancestors, the lumberjack, the wood person's ancestors, the conditions that came together to grow the tree in the first place, the parent tree, the tree's ancestors in the forest, the birds, insects, seasons, winds, and all the elements of earth, water, fire, wind, and space. Nothing exists on its own without an interdependence on everything else. Seeing and experiencing the world's interdependence is touching the absolute truth.

From the perspective of Contemplative Psychology, touching into absolute truth is touching the openness of our fundamental truth of nonduality. Our awareness of the interconnectedness of life, in a sense, is our Buddhahood, or our unconditioned enlightenment. This true nature is often described as the Sun, shrouded by the clouds of misperception. The ultimate truth allows us to see multiple perspectives of reality. Most of us can only glimpse these open interconnected experiences in micro-moments. We struggle to describe these experiences from the place of relative truth.

In dualistically divided consciousness, relative truth is steeped in the conditioning we bring to everything. At the same time, we navigate reality by this truth; for example, we are conditioned to know (thank goodness) that a red light is a universal sign to stop. There is capacity to perceive reality directly and accurately, but that requires the difficult and uncomfortable work of seeing through the conditioned reality of relative truth. Chögyam Trungpa explains, "Relative truth, or kundzop in Tibetan, is the phenomenal world, which is an outfit, a self-existing show. The phenomenal world is a performance, living theater. Relative truth is a show-off, a bluff. There is no substance, but there are still a lot of things going on. The relative world should not be looked down upon, however. This dressed-up world is actually very hard to work with. To realize the relative truth as truth, you need to transcend neurosis and psychosis. When you have become sane, you have experienced egolessness fully, you see that the real world is actually a real world. You see the world of reality completely and fully without any problem and any big deal."[37]

---

37 Trungpa, Chögyam, Realizing the Emptiness of Ordinary Reality, Part Five: Emptiness and Compassion, *The Bodhisattva Path of Wisdom and Compassion: The Profound Treasury of the Ocean of Dharma, Volume 2*, Leif, Judy editor. (Boston & London: Shambhala, 2001), pp. 150–151.

Shifting from observing the relative phenomenal experience of everyday life to accessing and understanding absolute truth is normally a process facilitated by realized Buddhist masters. However, the absolute nature of reality is not that lofty. Absolute nature is perceived through the simplicity of mind anytime we are not occupying all the space with ego. Gazing at the moon and stars, for example, brings us into a wider perspective of the universe and its inhabitants.

The real task in Contemplative Psychology, and in working with an exchange, is remembering the nature of these two truths. Expanding our minds enough to touch into the nondual aspect of exchange requires releasing our relative perspectives. Knowing about and discerning the two truths, relative and ultimate reality, is a necessary step in the journey of discovering our potency of the heart.

In Contemplative Psychology, joining the two truths is the process of integrating and joining with our intrinsic health. The journey begins, again and again, fresh on the meditation cushion. If we truly experience the space at the end of the out-breath, we touch into this unconditioned truth of open space, the ultimate truth. Then we come home to the relative on the in-breath, yet we don't necessarily have to become focused on the self. Each breath, in and out, invites further and further integration of space. We begin to see our thoughts like clouds, both insubstantial yet vivid in appearance and emotion, and return again and again to the solidity of the body and the fluidity and openness of the breath. Synchronizing body, breath, and mind, we are joining the two truths. Taking this kind of ease and relaxation into dialog to benefit others is the fruition of Contemplative Psychology; we call this fruit Compassionate Exchange.

In terms of navigating the two truths in everyday life, we do so by treading the path of mutual benefit when we honor the relative truth of emotional energy balanced with our unconditioned health and innate openness. The relative truth is the compass with which we navigate, and we aspire to maintain an unconditional view. When we work for others' benefit, self-care's relative conditions are unforgiving without a mutual journey of including ourselves.

CHAPTER X

Cultivating Compassionate Exchange

I began my career as a therapist working with white middle-class women suffering from issues of body dysmorphia and diagnosed with an eating disorder, either bulimia or anorexia nervosa. In other words, I was working with myself.

I began my therapeutic career at Boulder Memorial Hospital in Boulder, Colorado, which was a Seventh-day Adventist hospital. The Seventh-day Adventists have always been credited for their forward innovations in health care, and Boulder Memorial Hospital was one of the very first for-profit hospitals offering treatment of eating disorders that were escalating in American women, particularly those who were middle-class and white, along with the exercise fad, in the early 1980s. Over time, the approach of treating primarily middle-class women in in-patient clinics lost favor due to the high recidivism and refusal of insurance companies to foot the bill; the treatment yielded low efficacy.

However, from my first clinical therapeutic job at Boulder Memorial Hospital through a final position in my eating disorder career as the Clinical Director at Mt. Diablo Hospital in Walnut Creek,

California, I became very cynical toward for-profit psychiatric care due to the "heads in beds approach" to keeping a lucrative bottom line.

At age 27, I was far too young to be a therapist. At Boulder Memorial, I found myself comparing my personal history to the stories of my clients. I had the feeling my story was way worse than their stories. When I allowed myself to see my clients' experiences as parallel to my own, some part of my young therapeutic identity could not make sense of women just like me being pathologized and hospitalized. I'd done therapy for my eating disorder before being hired; however, on the continuum of recovery, I was far from healed. I always wondered what luck or karma it was that led me to be in the seat of the healer? The dichotomy just didn't make sense to me.

Merely living in Boulder, Colorado, in the early '80s meant attending and participating in a culture of "body thin and beautiful." Obsessions with losing weight and staying fit were not only expected, they were promoted at every turn. My daily exercise routine included bicycling, rock climbing, running, and working out in a gym, and it was not uncommon for me to attend more than one aerobics class daily. The anaerobic lifestyle was just starting to explode in the early '80s, along with an entire industry to treat the effects of this obsessive pursuit. Boulder, Colorado, was like a bulimic resort spa.

The women I found myself treating at Boulder Memorial described themselves as being raised in "dysfunctional families," as did I. That terminology was arriving on the therapeutic scene from the 12-step recovery domain, however, and I was coming from Contemplative Psychology training at Naropa with the indoctrination of intrinsic health. "Dysfunctional" anything to my ears was highly suspect.

As an early therapist, I found the quality of the relationships I established with my clients was the only thing I had to offer. I'd trained to be authentic and genuine at Naropa, and I shared a lot of myself, especially in the many topic-based groups I led with hospitalized women and their families. I worked to bring my fresh degree in Contemplative Psychotherapy into play in these clinical settings. I never had problems with the clients or their loved ones, but I struggled a great deal with antiquated ideas held by my colleagues.

One psychiatrist said to me, "When you speak to clients with your esoteric ideas of intrinsic health and basic sanity, these girls begin to think they're no longer sick. They're sick! Their eating disorders are pathological and you're doing them a great disservice." Had I the words to respond to my coworker at the time, I would have said that labeling others dysfunctional with clinical diagnosis seems akin to the way "borderline" or "histrionics" have been hurled at women from the dawn of psychotherapy. And while some people feel relieved when they find out that their brand of suffering has a name and that others also suffer from the same diagnosis, The Diagnostic Statistics Manual[38] has done a lot to obliterate all notions of intrinsic health.

That early professional experience sharpened the way I perceived the process of working with clients in a clinical environment. In the decades since, my belief in the value of the practice I studied at Naropa has deepened profoundly. Karuna Training is for anyone with an interest in Contemplative Psychology and Compassionate Exchange. We do not aim to produce therapists. However, many

---

38 *The Diagnostic and Statistical Manual of Mental Disorders* (DSM latest edition: DSM-5, publ. 2013) is a publication by the American Psychiatric Association (APA) for the classification of mental disorders using a common language and standard criteria.

therapists partake in our training. We train *contemplative care providers* who work in many professions, and we train people to be open and skillful in the practice of engaged compassion. In Karuna Training, we practice *mutual recovery* through the method of Compassionate Exchange. Mutual recovery can only occur in a relationship of equals. Even though one person may be acting as a compassionate friend, there is no hierarchy present.

In a Compassionate Exchange, we are mutually entering into an aspect of the healing process. As practitioners practicing this method, being part of the healing process doesn't mean our story is at the center of the conversation. That's the point; it doesn't matter whose story it is in a Compassionate Exchange, we are entering into a psychological and feeling process mutually. This journey is one of refining the mind's capacities into further awareness and personal resourcing. We find out that the potency of offering a microscopic truth is in our ability to open fully and entirely to intrinsic health. We then oscillate back home and feel the exchange, and with finesse and timing, we offer a reflection back to others in a way that is neither intrusive nor superficial. In Compassionate Exchange practice we simultaneously offer ourselves selflessly to another and release the habit of "othering" others, which means we let go of attachment to our interpretations, projections, and opinions.

This chapter explores Compassionate Exchange and how to use the practice as a means of *resourcing* ourselves along with benefiting others. Resourcing ourselves means we learn to draw on the innate strength and potency of the human heart. There is a need for this tender contact and connection, something the body integrates as human kindness, understanding, and a direct nurturance source. Nurturing ourselves through Compassionate Exchange is the path of *mutual recovery,* an approach whereby, as the Buddhists put it, "giver and receiver are one."

Compassionate Exchange Is Mutual Recovery

Compassionate Exchange is a ritual of leading our lives with our hearts fully open and awake. Living our lives in openness and generosity is born from refining the practice of mindfulness-awareness. Compassionate Exchange occurs in simple moments of presence. It is likewise a form of exercise, offering ourselves as compassionate friends to another person when requested. It is a way of life.

We strengthen our minds and open our hearts through the practice of Tonglen, taking and sending meditation, discussed earlier in this book. We practice exchanging self with others in our mind's eye and directly open to our own and others' suffering. In fact, the Mahayana Buddhist path encourages us to one-pointedly take the grit of our lives and learn to shine the jewel of our hearts. Tonglen is a time-tested method for awakening and ripening our innate compassion in relationships with one another. Eventually, we learn to exchange ourselves with others in conversation through the practice of Compassionate Exchange.

We practice Compassionate Exchange by refining our awareness in relationships with others. In Compassionate Exchange, there's an intention to listen and explore another's lived experience, and there's also the ability to evoke another's intrinsic health. Ultimately, as we learn to offer ourselves selflessly to others, we're tapping into the inseparable nature of our own and others' basic sanity.

To offer acceptance makes space and provides kindness for our own and others' personal experiences of pain. Creating space for pain is synonymous with self-healing. The foundational work of Compassionate Exchange has to do with our orientation to the present moment. We have already developed our ability to work with emotional energy with nonjudgmental awareness, and in general, we accept ourselves as we are, with all our horns, warts, and unwanted character traits and conditioning. Accepting ourselves as we are makes us more generous in accepting others.

Compassionate Exchange is how we extend ourselves to others and how we're mutually healed through the relationship of offering ourselves to others. When I was training to be a therapist in the early 1980s there was a taboo around the therapist sharing anything personal about themselves while working with others therapeutically. As if we were a blank slate, what we said and did as a therapist was meant to appear as if it came out of an unbiased mind and body.

Modern research has confirmed that the "relational stance" of the therapeutic practitioners, i.e., whether they be nurses, doctors, or therapists, with those they serve is the most critical component concerning positive outcomes in all types of healing relationships.[39] The relational stance entails the view from which the client is approached; if the provider views their clients as possessing basic sanity and resilience or whether they view them as the sum of their pathologies truly matters in the healing relationship.

We must remember that the field of psychotherapy and treatment for psychological illness is truly in its infancy comparative with other sciences such as biology, botany, and biological medicine and healing. Sigmund Freud's "talking therapy" only took hold in

---

39 DeAngelis, Tori, "Better Relationships with Patients Leads to Better Outcomes," American Psychiatric Association, online article, November 2019. "Based on its 16 meta-analyses on aspects of the therapy relationship, the APA Task Force on Evidence-Based Relationships and Responsiveness concludes that a number of relationship factors—such as agreeing on therapy goals, getting client feedback throughout the course of treatment and repairing ruptures—are at least as vital to a positive outcome as using the right treatment method."

the early 20th century. Behavioral medicine emerged as late as the 1970s with horrific reviews from its recipients. Stories of lobotomies and inhuman asylum environments can be conjured up for most of us when we think about the history of psychiatry and behavioral medicine.

Ed Podvoll stressed the dangers of therapists adopting what he called "asylum mentality." "Contact with insanity tends to provoke it . . . Asylum mentality is a mind of exerting power over others, in this case, 'therapeutic power.'"[40] These warnings penetrated deeply in my early years of therapeutic training, possibly because my family members had undergone psychiatric and alcohol treatment and experienced a lot of shame attached to those experiences.

In my early years as a clinician for eating disorders, I encountered a great deal of "asylum mentality," both in myself and in my colleagues. As I continued in my clinical career, working in nonprofit community-based settings to treat chronic mental illness, I found the "asylum mentality" to be even worse. Clinicians in such environments are likely to be undertrained and overworked. These facilities are insufficiently funded services and rely on government allotments. The bad taste in my mouth around treatment settings, both for-profit and community-based, probably has served the most to steer me toward training nonprofessionals in Contemplative Psychology.

I am encouraged to see other approaches to healing emphasizing health and basic sanity emerge in recent years. Therapeutic approaches such as client-centered therapy, or Rogerian work, and Dr. Martin Seligman's positive psychology, which studies a strength-

---

40 Podvoll, Edward, MD, *The Seduction of Madness: Revolutionary Insights into the World of Psychosis and a Compassionate Approach to Recovery at Home* (New York: Perennial, 1991), p. 62.

based approach to recovery and addressing psychological challenges, have become part of the variety of paths available to practitioners seeking training. The world is beginning to understand that a mutual relationship, a relationship of equals, is far more beneficial than a top-down traditional hierarchy in healing, in terms of attaining positive outcomes.

Refining Touch and Go

Contemplative Psychology requires we invest ongoing time in refining our awareness through mind-training. The mindfulness-awareness practice cultivates a nuanced awareness of our relationship to space, the energy of emotions, and other invisible powers of the universe. Sitting with ourselves in meditation, in some moments, we touch into the unbound open space of our innate nature with little to no self-consciousness. We experience a moment of vastness and relief.

The next moment in meditation, we're down a rabbit hole in our mind's eye, working on an old issue we've chewed through a thousand times before. We notice we're gone and gently touch the atmosphere of the mind's wandering. Then, with intention, we firmly exercise the muscle of mind by pulling ourselves back to the fresh open space of the present moment. Again and again, through this approach to "touch and go" on the meditation cushion, we cultivate a nonjudgmental awareness of the mind's wanderings, openings, closings, and vast spaciousness.

Compassionate Exchange practice invites us to use a "touch and go" approach to exchanging self with others. When working with others in whatever capacity, we tap into the shared nondual space of our innate openness and health. We then oscillate back home to take a temperature of our bodily sensations and reactions as a method of touching into the now of the present moment in ourselves. What is our exchange right now?

Actively oscillating back and forth between oneself and others helps to both regulate and integrate our present-moment experience. We are both increasing our intensity capacity to stay with difficult emotions. At the same time, we are grounding ourselves in our reactions and sensations while working with another's experience. "Touch and go" in Compassionate Exchange is especially helpful when working with another's state of mind or extreme emotions because it supports us in staying present and engaged.

By now, if we've established a practice of meditation, we've discovered the mind is naturally a wanderer. We have realized that following the mind down every path it takes or believing everything we think is usually not advantageous. Believing everything we think is also a challenge when we're communicating with others.

It's common to subliminally think things like, "That's a pretty impressive story he's telling; how do I compare to him?" We're thinking about our next response instead of deep listening. The shotgun style of listening anticipates, asks, "What will I say?" and serves to maintain a trigger-ready answer when there is a gap in the conversation. When doing this, we're listening with a well-trained "watcher" sitting on our shoulders, judging and comparing everything we and the others say in a continuum of who's on top, who's the best or the coolest in the hierarchy of the moment.

Learning how to show up without the baggage of a watcher, or the need to be right out of insecurity, is the accomplishment of learning to relax with ourselves as we are. Relaxing with ourselves as we are is what makes us excellent containers to practice Compassionate Exchange with others. This openness and presence in our capacity to listen to others is a path of self-healing, as well as tremendously beneficial to others.

Working with exchange and utilizing the method of "touch and go" are means to staying present and offering ourselves more selflessly in the act of listening. When we see ourselves straying off into a habitual comparative mind, we can touch the space of that, familiarizing ourselves with the energy and feeling of that pattern. Along the way, we notice it and instantly let go by releasing the watcher. That watcher is insecure and seeking sustenance and connection. Through our studies, we've found that, ironically, the watcher is cutting us off from the very intimacy we're seeking in our relationships.

Genuinely connecting with others non-self-consciously is meant to resource ourselves. When we feel trust and feel a connection to another, when we feel seen and heard, we are instantly resourced, filled up with that which we are continually seeking. When we don't know how to resource ourselves we're continually seeking gratification and nurturance from substances, food, drugs, alcohol, consuming things, and relationships. These substitutes for nurturance create an itch in us that cannot be scratched.

The only real way to resource ourselves is to be available and responsive enough in our interactions with others to receive sustenance and connection. Resourcing ourselves means we are not monitoring the situation constantly in our minds but instead are relaxed, open, and trustful with ourselves in a relationship with another.

Working in Compassionate Exchange with the approach of "touch and go" is naturally resourcing for us. We integrate the truth of our experience by oscillating back and forth between the experience of complete openness and connection with another and back to the knowledge of how it's showing up in our body, speech, and mind through the exchange.

I think of oscillation as a bit like *chuckling*, which is a rocking motion that is familiar in some Jewish traditions. Chuckling is the practice during davening (reciting a prayer) of rocking back and forth while reading the Torah, a kind of embodiment of the prayer. Oscillation is a similar process, though it happens internally.

We use the consciousness of "touch and go" in order to integrate the two truths of our experience, the relative and the absolute. Integrating these two truths within ourselves through oscillation is the way to be genuinely present to all dimensions of ourselves, present with our whole being—a fully embodied and conscious presence. "Touch and go" is the embodiment of Compassionate Exchange work.

Three Phases of Developing a Bodhisattva's Heart

Bodhisattvas are the Buddhist representation of a being capable of selfless Compassionate Exchange in every moment. We're borrowing from Buddhism with this high example in the path of training in Contemplative Psychology. Bodhisattvas know how to use the grit of their existence to polish the jewels of who others are. They dedicate themselves to benefiting others, putting others before themselves, and offering themselves in Compassionate Exchange in all interactions.

It is important to grasp what it means to put others before ourselves. From a Contemplative Psychology perspective, compassion is the ultimate expression of a desire to alleviate the suffering of others through exchanging oneself with another. Giving ourselves away selflessly to others is not about becoming a doormat for someone else, not unless becoming a doormat is the most beneficial and wise thing to do in the moment. For example, we may need to become a doormat if it provides a stepping-stone back to practical reality. I learned a lot about this kind of offering as the director of that mental health crisis house, working with people who were suffering from acute psychosis.

In the safe house, we had a rule that when people came to stay, even for one night, they had to shower, put whatever belongings they had away, make their bed, and, when possible, help the house with chores. When people first arrived, often in the middle of the night and police escorted, they'd be hella angry. In this situation, one had to offer oneself as what might be considered a doormat, an absorber of greatly suffering new clients' heavy emotional footfalls, to assist them in stabilizing enough to receive the assistance the house had to offer. Not personalizing people's insults or anger, and at the same time laying down the rules, gently and firmly, with tough love.

The altruistic aspiration to be of benefit is a natural impetus within all of us, but due to conditioning and the fast pace of everyday life, this impetus of love, kindness, and desire to help must be cultivated through constant refinement on the path of life.

The Bodhisattva is an embodiment of both wisdom and compassion, meaning that the head and the heart join in all acts and expressions of compassion. From a Buddhist perspective, it's said that genuine compassion, nondual compassion, is as rare as a star in the daytime.[41]

---

41 Rinpoche, Patrul, *The Words of My Perfect Teacher* (Boston & London: Shambhala, 1998).

We can contemplate what simple acts of kindness we enacted in the last week. I sent a book as a gift to my sister, but did I do so selflessly or because, on some level, I want her to look up to me as the learned older sister? These subtleties of egoic motivation hide everywhere, and when we discover them, it's good news because it means we are honest with ourselves. Honestly, seeing the subtleties of our self-deception is one of the most challenging stages of developing a Bodhisattva heart.

The word *compassion* must be distinguished from words like *empathy*, *sympathy*, and *charity*. All these words express caring and extending oneself to others, but one factor is that they are all still dualistic in their definition, meaning they arise out of "this and that." When we say we feel empathy, we are still distinguished as someone feeling the emotions of another. The word *sympathy* expresses a subtle, or sometimes not so subtle, hierarchy. The sympathetic person has something the other doesn't and feels sad that the other has less than we do. Charity is the enactment of hierarchical sympathy. These are tricky states that insist we always investigate our microscopic motivation in our actions toward others. Do we genuinely aspire to benefit or are we putting on a role we think we should inhabit?

Traditionally there are three stages to developing a Bodhisattva's potent compassionate heart. The first stage is the **self-healing stage.** Self-healing occurs when we stop torturing ourselves for being ourselves and make friends with ourselves as we are. From a Contemplative Psychology perspective, we need to make friends with ourselves fully before being genuinely helpful to others. Again, this is a cultural artifact today that professionally trained youth are degreed and certified, supposedly ready to jump into a healing profession before the heart muscles have evolved. One needs a lot of strength of heart to truly open to the pain of others.

The second stage of developing a compassionate heart is a long phase called **"taking our fences down."** The second stage can be studied in our communication and interactions with others. This stage requires disciplined patience and trust in allowing others in. We all have different barometers in how open we are and how close we allow others. Some of us carry traumatic injuries in our bodies that we are not fully conscious of, which serve to defend us from others who pose a subtle potential threat. Often, we are not aware of our conditioned defenses.

Offering ourselves in Compassionate Exchange is automatically an act of taking down our fences. We must be responsive and available in this practice, which requires us to open. Letting down our fences by no means is giving up our boundaries. We must see what and who we are offering ourselves to with clarity. We don't need a fortress to open; we need a safe container. The measure of safety is different for everyone, and sensitivity to trauma is very important.

Often when Karuna students first sit down as a "compassionate friend" for another person in the more formal practice of Compassionate Exchange, they express a lot of anxiety and fear. Their main worry is they will do something wrong. This worry is an expression of their watcher and possibly deep conditioning in not trusting themselves. Our self-conscious watcher doesn't want to let down the fences because we fear being seen as incompetent and vulnerable. There are multiple examples of emotional conditioning that support us in staying defined. The path of Contemplative Psychology is learning to identify one's fences and slowly dissolve them through trust in basic sanity, approaching oneself with loving-kindness (maitri) and opening and becoming responsive toward others as a means of resourcing oneself.

The third stage of developing one's bodhicitta is **developing our inner Bodhisattva** by practicing Bodhisattva activities. Traditionally becoming a Bodhisattva is marked by a ceremony of proclaiming our aspiration to grow our bodhicitta by using the grit of our existence as the path. In this stage, one has complete confidence in our own and others' intrinsic health, and yet there are layers to uncover in fully cultivating the heart's potential.

We grow our bodhicitta (awakened heart) through acts of love and compassion, and these acts accumulate in the potency of the heart. Maitri, loving-kindness, is our strength of mind. We touch this loving-kindness in micro-moments and recognize them as such. We might see the sweet smile of a baby or experience the boundless bright blue sky, or it can be anything that opens our hearts unconditionally. Unconditionally means the heart is unfiltered in that moment, fully naked, responsive, and available. In this practice, giver and receiver are one, meaning it is as essential to offer love and kindness as it is to receive love and compassion. Both giving and receiving are acts of generosity.

It needs to be said that in Contemplative Psychology, what we value most is our vulnerability; this is a tender-hearted way of discovering our strength. The practice of Compassionate Exchange is incredibly tender-hearted; it is a path that enables us to learn both to offer and to receive. We offer ourselves unconditionally to others, open, awake, and responsive to others' pain. We receive by allowing in the micro-moments of Compassionate Exchange. In Compassionate Exchange, we cultivate a potent heart while resourcing ourselves simultaneously.

We are starting with the traditional training of developing the limitless qualities of heart: maitri (loving-kindness), compassion, and sympathetic joy. Through these capacities of heart, we aspire to grow and strengthen our relative bodhicitta. As we gain strength, we experience the opened awakened unconditional heart space of absolute bodhicitta in micro-moments through "touch and go." This complete experience of bodhicitta is the fourth limitless quality, equanimity.

This means of cultivating Compassionate Exchange through developing our bodhichitta makes us very brave and beneficial toward others. Compassionate Exchange is the fruition of Contemplative Psychology.

SECTION THREE

Mining the Experience
of "Not One, Not Two"

CHAPTER XI

Every Relationship Matters

S ection three defines Contemplative Psychology's understanding of our true nature, openness (or egolessness). While continuing to apply the fundamental practices of Mahayana Buddhism, which includes mindfulness-awareness meditation and Tonglen, we begin to glimpse a more spacious accepting mind. We begin to experience a broader and more poignant knowing. We call this knowing *prajna*, a Sanskrit word meaning *discriminating-awareness wisdom*.

Prajna develops through contemplating the *paramitas* and especially applying these traits to our relationships. Paramitas are the vehicles we use to cross over the great river of selfishness to offer ourselves nondual compassion. The paramitas, in general, are a cascading set of principles to live by and thus awaken our bodhicitta. The paramitas are considered stepping-stones that lead toward an awakened and intelligent heart, but not out of striving toward a goal, much more by allowing the emotional waves of awareness to wear away the rough and ragged ego walls. The process is more one of simplifying than of striving toward an end goal.

Paramitas serve to dissolve ego's habits gently, and we begin to open to experiencing *things as they are* in a vaster context of knowing. Once a student said to me, "Those are big words you're using, 'things as they are.'" He was right; seeing phenomena free from the ego's perspective is beyond conventional seeing. For example, prajna always sees through the lens of the three marks of existence: impermanence, suffering, and non-self (egolessness). We generally don't keep the three marks of existence in our mind, but instead, we see things from a more conventional individualistic perspective.

We're discovering, in applying Contemplative Psychology methods, to be comfortable with the discomfort of not knowing. Not knowing is challenging because we fear it leaves us vulnerable. We feel exposed. Ed Podvoll said, "Contemplative Psychology is living in naked reality."[42] We open to the nakedness we share; we find the resources, the richness is in the shadows, and often uncomfortable feelings within us we are avoiding. We cannot avoid these spaces when we sit down on the meditation cushion and feel ourselves in the present moment. Engaged compassion requires us to step further and further into the groundlessness of not knowing, all the while staying awake, open, and systemically aware.

The groundless space of nondual compassion is evoked through rousing bodhicitta and cutting through to open space. We are encouraged to discover these micro-moments of the awakened heart in very ordinary experiences of everyday life. Most of the time, we miss these moments of connection because we're too consumed with ourselves.

---

42 Author's handwritten notes from Psychopathology class with Dr. Ed Podvoll at Naropa Institute, circa 1981.

Working in groundlessness requires a stable mind, seeing clearly, and a profound nonreferential mind. A nonreferential mind is a mind that easily rests in not knowing. To do so involves *intensity capacity* and the bravery to stay with vulnerability. Practicing this gentle form of *intensification practice* is gradually learning to stay with discomfort and potentially invites *transmutation*, the capacity to burn through our confusion with one-pointed awareness. We stay embodied and present with emotional energy and/or confusion and, suddenly (or not), the confusion dawns as wisdom.

In this section, we explore Contemplative Psychology's fruition, which is no less than full realization. Paradoxically, we should not seek realization but, instead, realization dawns spontaneously out of letting all hope of fruition go. Like the bright sun that emerges suddenly from behind a shrouded sky, mind's confusion suddenly clears, and in that nanosecond, we see and touch our potency of heart in nondual compassion.

In this chapter, Every Relationship Matters, we consider the challenges and opportunities of relationships through the lens of the Six Paramitas. Paramita is a Sanskrit word meaning "perfection" or "completeness." The Paramitas refers to how we cultivate our open-heartedness through our relationships, how we let down our fence. The Six Paramitas include the human traits of generosity, discipline, patience, exertion, and meditation, and all of those culminate in *prajnaparamita*. Prajnaparamita is said to be the "mother of all the Buddhas" because this is what births our Buddhahood, or awakened heart.

Deep and personal contemplation of the quality of our everyday relationships is valuable. The meaningful relationships, those we've killed off in our mind, and all the relationships we actively ignore bear tremendous fruit as we discover our challenges on the path of rousing an awakened heart. Every casual and purposeful relationship presents an opportunity to engage our profundity of heart. At the same time, we need to know how our relational habits are challenges to living engaged compassion.

From a Buddhist Psychology perspective, reality is living, coevolving, and arising out of our moment-to-moment choices of how we conduct ourselves in our body, speech, and mind with one another. Our choices, reactions, and simple words all impact other aspects of life on the planet and in the universe. Nothing is predestined but instead unfolding out of numerous causes and conditions ripening in the present moment. Understanding and integrating our interconnected nature on a global scale helps us realize that it does matter how we conduct ourselves and how every relationship matters.

Generosity Paramita

Before I studied Contemplative Psychology and entered the Buddhist path, I lived my life in crisis or near crisis for most of my teenage and young adult years. I felt a deep sense of not having enough, despite the fact that I was a "trust-fund baby." Not that I had enormous wealth, but enough, and if I had chosen to raise my gaze, I might have realized how privileged I was. Considering my dawning awareness of white privilege, this story now seems absurd to me. However, growing up in the '70s, we white folks did not dare to venture into our responsibility in the story of oppression of African Americans or any other indigenous or people of color.

The *not enough mentality* that I led my life with became most evident in my Contemplative Psychology study when I realized how difficult it was to open myself to others—whether in intimate relationships, friendships, or even simple gestures of helping others in the community such as giving up a seat on the bus to an elder or picking up trash that I didn't make. The simple acts of opening to others were not even a consideration for me.

Chögyam Trungpa named this mind frame as a *poverty mentality*, the inability to open and give up even an ounce of what you think you possess. I recognized my poverty mentality arose from deep conditioning, perhaps due to my Depression-era parents; who knows? I found the antidote to my poverty was contemplating and enacting generosity, first toward myself.

"So the basic idea of generosity or the paramita of generosity," Trungpa tells us, "is learning how to part with the things that you have. You could be a beggar or you could be a millionaire, but it is still the mentality of poverty. You do not want to part with anything. Even if you have nothing to part with in terms of physical material, there is a fundamental basic state of mind that says that you should keep what you have, including your aggressions or passions or whatever you have: Just keep it, you might need it later."[43]

The first thing I had to give up on my journey to opening my heart was the extreme self-hatred I enacted toward my body. Making friends with my body entailed letting go of being a dancer and standing in front of mirrors, comparing my body to other women. Ironically, it was looking for a dance class that led me to Naropa Institute. I discovered my "self-healing stage" on the path as I learned to experience past trauma directly instead of taking out the pain on

---

43 Trungpa, Chögyam, *Paramita Practice* from the 1975 Hinayana Mahayana Seminary Transcripts (Boulder, CO: Vajradhatu Press, 1976), p. 268.

myself and my body. Now I can see that my inability to open to others was internalized trauma, perseverating fears, and unconscious wounding.

What I began to realize in contemplating generosity is that generosity was simply noticing and being open to others' pain instead of just my own. My self-healing started when I recognized that I was not available or trusting when consumed with myself. I was not available when obsessing over my weight, looks, lack of confidence, or feelings of unworthiness.

There are layers of experiences that reveal how awareness begins to dawn, and the first thing is making space and being generous with ourselves. In Contemplative Psychology, we start with our unique environments. We only must raise our gaze to see what kind of space we create for ourselves, as a seed of generosity, to begin our contemplation on generosity.

Things like setting the table and cleaning up after ourselves is an act of kindness and generosity toward ourselves. I remember, when I was a new meditator, a Naropa teacher once said, "Your environment reflects the state of your mind." I immediately went home and recognized that if that was true, then my mind was very claustrophobic. I spent the following few hours clearing things away and opening space in my room. I picked up my clothes, made my bed, and noticed for once that I had space to breathe. I felt better.

My newfound generosity toward myself in my environment began to spill over into my relationship with others. I was living as a nanny at the time with a family where the wife had suffered a severe bicycle accident and paralyzed her left side. When I interviewed for the position, she was in the hospital, and once I began my work as a nanny for her two young boys and husband, she returned home from the hospital. Her transition home was extremely difficult, and she was not happy to have a stranger in her house taking care of her family. She tried to take her own life on two occasions while I was living in the house; the second suicide attempt prompted me to quit my position as the family's nanny. I tried to maintain contact with her sons, but it was too difficult for everyone.

Naropa required that we attend a process group during this time, and there I was forced to explore the teachings as they landed in my everyday life. After complaining to the group that I felt victimized in this family by the wife, the group's response made me realize how much suffering this woman lived. I had to taste my lack of openness and generosity toward her pain. The reflection of the group made me see how selfish it was to maintain any territory. I felt victimized due to simply inheriting this crisis as the nanny instead of relating to the tragedy as it was.

Selfishness is the fruit of the poverty mentality; we are not available or open toward others, even when they're in severe pain in front of our eyes due to our obsession with that which we lack. In the few short months I lived with this family, I practiced generosity paramita by opening to the wife's suffering, which was difficult in the face of her aggression toward me. Through contemplating the paramita of generosity, I was able to open my heart and let go of my entitlement and pain enough to taste and feel the immense suffering of another person.

I will be forever grateful for the gift she offered me, the paralyzed wife who suffered so much loss. She provided me liberation from my poverty mentality, enough for me to witness her suffering. Generosity toward another suffering is the first step in *letting down our fences* discussed in chapter VIII. We begin to see and feel another's pain. Our self-obsessions and habits of mind start to dissolve through this outward awareness when we're generous toward another's suffering in a relationship.

Discipline Paramita

Generosity naturally leads to the next paramita, which is discipline. Taking down our fences and being responsive to another person in pain requires a certain amount of relational intelligence. This kind of intelligence understands that remaining open requires sustenance, along with the type of resourcing that arises from simplifying our relationship to one another. The paramita of discipline is about simply acting appropriately, conducting oneself with minimal drama. Discipline paramita teaches us how to keep things simple.

I'm writing this chapter on the first anniversary of the COVID-19 pandemic, March 11, 2021. I've spent an entire year at home with my new husband, socially isolating and, for the most part, free from travel. This year together with him and my geriatric pug had many blessings, and it's also been too much togetherness. The nonstop togetherness has tested our relationship in ways that have illuminated the discipline paramita, so necessary in all intimate relationships.

Before the pandemic, my marriage was balanced by my continuous travel schedule. I was only home intermittently about four months of the entire year. When the lockdown occurred in March 2020, my husband and I found ourselves very much on top of one another. Now on the first anniversary, we've survived due to our relationship to discipline.

We have had to learn to offer a lot of space to one another and keep a fundamental ritualized structure to our daily lives during this stressful and claustrophobic time. We do a great deal together, and we also spend a lot of time in the house apart, balancing being open to one another, courteous, thoughtful, and most importantly, not being enmeshed. The exercise in proper conduct has required space awareness, mindfulness of one another's needs, and respectfully maintaining space for oneself.

Finding discipline is a balancing act and undoubtedly necessary in all intimate relationships. Discipline is also profoundly enhancing in our everyday relationships as well. We could say discipline is about cleaning up after ourselves. It's like doing your dishes and making your bed, and not because your mother told you to be "good," but because it's an act of offering space and consideration for others.

Discipline also requires us to taste our loneliness. We are born alone, we live alone, and we die alone, and no relationship can make that be otherwise. Putting expectations and demands on others to make us feel whole, cared for, or any other thing that tries to use relationships to alleviate our aloneness's truth is lacking in the paramita of discipline. One of the most joyful factors in learning to accept and even appreciate our loneliness is respecting others' and our own space.

Patience Paramita

Generosity and discipline paramitas open us to the needs of ourselves and others, yet we still have many damaging resentments, irritations, and complaints that confuse us and congest our hearts in relationships. One of the most challenging aspects of letting down our fences to rouse our bodhicitta is decolonizing the mind's hierarchy on who matters and who doesn't.

Generosity and discipline bring us to the paramita of patience, which dissolves the subtle and not-so-subtle scraggly conditioning of aggression. Patience paramita is not about waiting in line patiently and taking our turn politely; it's much more about tilling the layers of forbearance, which serves to wear away our entitlement and righteousness.

I'm a very impatient person by nature and sometimes annoyed by ordinary everyday tasks, especially if they take too much time, like calling a bank if there is suspected fraud, figuring out an unknown charge on a credit card bill, or contacting a business helpline and being put on hold. I hate to wait, and my impatience can show up as intolerance and blatant annoyance in speaking to those unfortunate people who screen and answer customer calls all day long. I've learned to aspire to be kind to those unknown people in practicing the paramita of patience.

Addressing my privilege and aggressive entitlement on the phone in seeming anonymity is a form of decolonizing the hierarchy in our heads around who does and doesn't matter in a relationship. In practicing the patience paramita, we notice when impatience and aggression begin to emanate from us toward others, and we investigate those moments when we decide certain people do not matter. We can say and act any way we want because we don't know these people. We have established a hierarchy of some people being less critical in our minds than others.

This hierarchy of relationships may not even be conscious, but if we apply curiosity to our aggression in relationships, we may find that we are usually number one in our minds. We are angry because we are the most critical person in the composition at any time, and what we think, say, or do is right. Aggression thrives on justification, and impatience arises in relationships because we've decided there are people we do not see as important enough to warrant our respect or kindness.

Privilege sports entitlement in terms of how we approach relationships; we only need to investigate our past and current relationships with authorities, like bosses, parents, and people for whom their respect is something that mattered. We may have another hierarchy in place with our partners, our children, and perhaps people in our close and distant families. We treat grocery stores and bank workers with courtesy, if we know them or when we're in a good mood.

As we explore this aspect of ourselves, we can learn a great deal from spending a day contemplating patience paramita in all of our various relationships, observing how we manifest irritation, outright frustration, and aggression, along with forbearance, respect, and thoughtfulness in our relationships. Patience paramita tends to reveal the unspoken and often unconscious hierarchies we've arranged in our minds in our relationships.

Exertion Paramita

Looking deeply into these conditioned hierarchies we've set up in our mind takes the paramita of exertion. When we contemplate more deeply these relational hierarchies, we discover our unconscious biases being acted out in relationships. Exertion paramita, despite its name, doesn't always mean we have to do something; it might mean doing nothing but sitting, feeling, and contemplating more deeply. In a relationship, practicing exertion paramita is staying with painful awareness and feeling it more deeply, maybe even feeling it more deeply through exchanging self with others, as we do in Tonglen.

As Chögyam Trungpa explains, "The definition of exertion is a sense of not giving up. And the nature of exertion is being delighted in the practice, delightfulness in the practice . . . exertion is simply continuing what has happened already in the three previous paramitas. It is continuing that way, just going on that way, and there is a delight in continuing and being patient. And, if you figure it out, if you put together generosity, discipline, and patience, they actually amount to exertion and delight in what we are doing."[44]

The past summer of 2020, with the murder of George Floyd at the hands of police and the awareness of Black Lives Matter protests coming further into mainstream consciousness, there was a new historical awareness of the pain of Black Americans and people of color all over the world who struggle with white supremacy and systemic racism. As a white person, a person who practices Contemplative Psychology, a person who teaches Compassionate Exchange, I experienced this rising awareness as a global reckoning, made even more poignant with the COVID-19 pandemic.

I'm 64 years old while writing this, and I've been studying the multiple manifestations of civil rights, anti-racism, and diversity training since seventh grade. Still, I found my ignorance and lack of awareness over the years toward Black peoples' plight a humbling and alarming truth.

---

44 Trungpa, Chögyam, *Paramita Practice* from the 1975 Hinayana Mahayana Seminary Transcripts (Boulder, CO: Vajradhatu Press, 1976), p. 270.

My contemplations invited me into the discipline of "staying with it" and applying myself further into the pain of the situation. This required stepping beyond simply blaming the police, politicians, and laws that discriminate in order to see exactly how my conduct, speech, and mental beliefs contribute to the pain. This exercise has taken a lot of exertion!

Exertion paramita has been sustaining me in my relationship with white friends who do not necessarily want to look or feel deeply about social inequalities due to privileging whiteness. I've come to understand that society evolves its social awareness through repetition and permeating the environment. Like waves in the ocean, awareness comes in a succession of repetitive shocks that serves to widen and liberate our conditioned consciousness of any given social commentary. Awakening to our social blindness is dependent on how willing we are to stay with discomfort. That is where exertion paramita comes in—we learn to stay with what we don't know and what others don't know, even though it can be frustrating.

To awaken to the truths of my white supremacy requires me to be even more generous, more disciplined with whom I read and with whom I study, and more patient with the entire dilemma we currently face. Exertion is what propels me to stay genuinely open to the pain.

Visionaries such as Starla Lewis, the Rev. angel Kyodo williams, and Lama Rod Owens, all Black-bodied teachers generous enough to help people wake up to systemic racism, have helped me stay with the bottomless pain and unanswerable suffering of being Black in America and how I've contributed. Only through the paramita of exertion can I dare to let down my fences enough to see, and to look further into how my privilege impacts my relationships with all people of color.

The paramita of exertion is necessary for discerning and feeling our responsibility to our relationship with society in general. We are each a cog in the collective wheel of the whole and interconnected through significant and seemingly insignificant relationships in every moment.

Meditation Paramita

Contemplating the paramitas regarding relationships is helpful medicine for awakening our heart potential and growing our bodhicitta around societal awareness. There is another ingredient to add to the soup of engaged, compassionate practice, to aid us in developing stability, clear-seeing, and a profound strength of mind. Without the paramita of meditation, we're not mindful or clear-seeing enough to notice the contrasts and nuances of passion, aggression, and ignorance we're employing in our relationships. Mindfulness is the fruit of the paramita of meditation.

As we do this work, we become mindful of how we are impacting others in relationships and how they are impacting us. Our exaggerated egoic antics can be embarrassing, but because we have practiced maitri and self-healing in Contemplative Psychology, we can apply meditation paramita as prescribed mindfulness to our experience and be gentler and even-minded. When we slow down and notice, we don't have to act out, and we don't have to suppress our feelings; we can just see them as they are arising.

To feel and stay with the pain of our habits in relationships, we need the strength of mind. Meditation paramitas instill this strength of mind to hold our minds steady, even when we don't feel like it. If someone yells at us or misbehaves, we don't indulge our pain by hurling back another insult. We use our practice on the cushion to apply a measured and nonjudgmental openness to all experiences, whether we like the experience or not. In doing this, we cultivate equanimity.

Until we learn to apply the last paramita, however, we arise out of the relative truth conditioned by how things appear versus how they are.

Prajnaparamita

It's easy to realize how the previously discussed paramitas of generosity, discipline, patience, exertion, and meditation work collaboratively with each other, tilling the ground of our confusion and awakening our heart through being touched and vulnerable in our relationships with others. The first five are said to be like a river that flows into the ocean of the final paramita, prajnaparamita. Chögyam Trungpa defined prajna as a "clear perception of the phenomenal world."[45]

Prajnaparamita is aligned with the principle of shunyata, emptiness, or unbound openness. Prajna is what sees through ego's illusions and is incredibly liberating when we apply its discriminating-awareness wisdom to our relationships, whether intimate or societal. For example, when we find ourselves in the middle of a heated fight with our loved one, we suddenly raise our gaze enough to see that we are full of ego, territoriality, and righteousness. Prajna sees through this the natural emptiness of all situations that are solidified with ego's games. It draws on generosity, discipline, patience, exertion, and

---

45 Trungpa, Chögyam, *Paramita Practice* from the 1975 Hinayana Mahayana Seminary Transcripts (Boulder, CO: Vajradhatu Press, 1976), p. 271.

meditation to pierce through delusion. Prajnaparamita is said to be the mother of all the Buddhas, giving birth to our realization and revealing the diamonds within us.

Applying the paramitas to our everyday relationships offers us a lifetime of practice. In Contemplative Psychology, since we concern ourselves with awakening our heart and practicing nondual compassion in Compassionate Exchange, the relationship vehicle is an excellent mirror into the paramita practices.

Working with paramitas is a circular process, whereby we notice our openness or lack of it through our ability to be generous. We become disciplined by keeping things spacious and straightforward and open our eyes for the subtle and not-so-subtle aggressions; that is, applying patience paramita. Again and again, we stay with whatever intensity arises from our discovery. By using exertion, we expand our intensity capacity to be vulnerable. Over and over returning to the meditation cushion, we experience further stability through meditation, and we widen our awareness. Prajna is born in glimpses of working with the paramitas with all we encounter, and we awaken our heart in bodhicitta.

Prajnaparamita dawns like the sun from behind the shrouded sky. It's a penetrating experience that imprints a certain kind of knowing, a nonreferential knowing. The higher knowing of prajna focuses our journey of awakening through the practice of Compassionate Exchange.

CHAPTER XII

The Sword and the Fan

When I was in my early 20s, I became fascinated with the high desert Canyonlands of Utah. I decided to test myself by backpacking in the Canyonlands Wilderness Reserve in late spring. I started in Moab, a dusty dot on the highway with a tiny motel, one bar, and a post office. I purchased a small book titled *Geography of the Canyonlands* in a gas station on my way into the Canyonlands.

I don't remember too much about the trip except being afraid at night, significant blisters, and I think I came back earlier than I planned. I remember reading the small geological book while sitting by a creek, shadowed by ancient tall canyon walls, reading how the place I was seated had previously been an ocean, a desert, a lush plain, etc. I meditated on the Canyonlands, how impermanent the earth is, and how small we humans are in geological time. The last page of the book said if the Canyonlands' lifespan was the length of your arms stretched out, then in geological time, human beings had inhabited the canyons the slice of your middle fingernail. I read that passage a few times to let it in and experienced the vastness of time and space and human significance considering that. Being in those canyons alone widened my mind considerably about human impact and consequences on the planet.

When our mind expands beyond our habituated "relative" perspectives, we can see a greater picture of "things as they are"; that is, we apply and experience prajnaparamita, the birth of the Buddha-mind and a momentary capacity to touch into absolute truth. Of course, to make sense of absolute truth, we must engage and integrate those experiences with the relative truth of ourselves at that moment as well. Developing the ability to join relative and absolute truth is how we become skillful with prajna. Contemplative Psychology concerns itself with the perception of the world and with cultivating a view of reality infused with shunyata, or emptiness. Whenever we point to egolessness, the mind naturally short-circuits—the very inference of emptiness renders ego inoperative. Contemplative Psychology is a path that disrupts conceptualization, an approach that has more to do with dissolving ideas of ourselves than trying to change or improve ourselves. We are perfect as we are if we can dissolve the conditioning that shrouds that perfection.

We naturally possess a pulsing heart of compassion, full of capacities to befriend ourselves and benefit others. Along the way, we learn to assume full responsibility for our mind's power and discern reality, decipher a more comprehensive view of things instead of the standard conceptualized versions of reality in which we are primarily perceiving. Contemplative Psychology is about coming home to ourselves as we are instead of who we think we should be.

This chapter elaborates on prajnaparamita, the culmination of the paramitas. Prajna works in concert with *compassion* to produce skillful means, known in Buddhist texts as *mahakaruna*, or great compassion. Great compassion is the fruition of Compassionate

Exchange. To put it simply, training the mind turns our allegiance to space or openness rather than to any particular conceptual constructs.

Mahakaruna and Emptiness

In general, Buddhist psychology and Buddhism use words and language to point to mental processes that are not easily articulated. We aspire not to get lost in the tangle of conceptualizations; however, it's important to understand we're in the process of cultivating that which is naturally within us already. The contemplative process incubates the loving nature within us. In Contemplative Psychology, we are growing our capacity to integrate an absolute perspective while developing away from our mental conditioning of selfishness. Contemplative processes take time and repetition, which serve to wear out egoic tendencies of the mind.

The primary principle of awakening the heart is living up to our most full capacity as human beings, capable of putting others' feelings and well-being first, seeing a much bigger picture, and able to remain in equanimity as a result. Leading with love, compassion, joy, and equanimity is the fruit of dissolving egoic territory. The seed of bodhicitta, which comprises love, compassion, joy, and equanimity, is a maternal instinct that exists within every sentient being, regardless of sex, or even when they are vicious and ferocious animals. The heart's potential is bodhicitta.

To engage these limitless qualities of the heart, we need methods and safe containers to practice. Over and over, we strengthen the capacities of our minds and turn their allegiance toward basic sanity. Contemplative methods such as mindfulness-awareness, Tonglen, the Four-Step Practice to stay with emotional intensity, and Maitri Space Awareness are a skillful means by which we till the ground of our loving hearts. Contemplative methods are the skillful means of Contemplative Psychology, and with these methods, we are mining for the diamonds within us.

Mahakaruna, or great compassion, arises from shunyata, or egolessness. As Trungpa puts it, "Great compassion becomes a source of great genuineness."[46] Mahakaruna is a regenerative resource that arises from living with an open heart, especially when we meet the hard truths of existence. Life presents us with continual paradoxes, difficult choices that need to be held with mahakaruna, a combination of skillful means and compassion. The practices of Contemplative Psychology help us to become vessels of maximum benefit in the world and society.

Compassionate Exchange practice offers a glimpse into the tenets of mahakaruna, enough so that we begin to question. With inquiry and curiosity, we begin to investigate, loosen, and disassemble how we habitually perceive reality. When we start to develop a vast perspective on reality while maintaining an open heart of compassion, this skillful means brings about the emergence of mahakaruna. Mahakaruna occurs when prajna and compassion are joined within us.

In the mid-1990s, I was fortunate to be married in the Zen Buddhist Mandala Garden of Green Gulch Farms in Muir Beach, California. The garden's circular shape is a mandala of California native plants and flowers, idyllic for marriage but rarely permitted as a venue

---

46 Trungpa, Chögyam, *Paramita Practice* from the 1975 Hinayana Mahayana Seminary Transcripts (Boulder, CO: Vajradhatu Press, 1976), p. 268.

(at least at that time). I married a man who had access to Green Gulch due to having been an apprentice monk and having tilled that garden under the renowned late horticulturist Alan Chadwick. Chadwick introduced the techniques of biodynamic farming at Green Gulch Zen Center.

The wedding ceremony we performed had been written by Chögyam Trungpa for advanced students on the Shambhala Path of Warriorship, to which my husband and I both were committed. The ceremony combined elements of Japanese, Tibetan, and Shambhala principles. During the ceremony, the bride and groom compose and spontaneously recite a devotional poem for one another. The ceremony's ritual proclamations were said to bind the couple's spiritual paths together *forever*, with the sole purpose to benefit others. As someone from a long lineage of divorce, the notion of *forever* was daunting, and yet I was clear I loved this man unconditionally.

Thus, on a bright blue Northern California October day, we gathered our guests in the sacred garden mandala. The garden was full of old friends and acquaintances, many Zen students from the San Francisco Zen community, and a couple of famous beat poets, and the affair was also a bit of a reunion. The atmosphere was charged with excitement.

During the ceremony, the bride offers her husband a fan, representing fanning the heart of compassion, a symbol of gentleness and feminine principle. The man offers his wife a sword, a symbol of prajna, discriminating-awareness wisdom, intuitive insight, skillful means, and masculine principle. In Tibetan Vajrayana Buddhism, the joining of masculine and feminine principles is an aspiration. The intention of joining masculine and feminine principles is to manifest skillful means, regardless of gender identity. Thus, when prajna and compassion join, synchronization of the head and the heart occur, or a union of intelligence and compassion. Without joining the head and the heart, we cannot see clearly, know what is, or know how to act with purpose.

When we ceremonially exchanged the fan and the sword under the bright blue NorCal sky, I catapulted out of my body a hundred feet above the ceremony, dissociating, yes, but remaining fully present somehow. The experience did not feel like a trauma response but some sort of intensification of that moment. I was out of my body, looking down on everyone in the circular garden from 100 feet above. The bird's-eye view image remains clear in my mind to this day.

At the moment, I could see the truth of the three marks of existence imprinted on everything and everyone: impermanence, suffering, and non-self. Specifically, I saw the fatal future of my marriage, and in fact, I could see that my husband and I had taken some sort of potent vow, like this one, many times already on a path of awakening. I could see all of this very clearly in a micro-moment of bodhicitta, and as painful as the recognition was, I could also see the perfection of the moment. The ability to hold heartbreak, confusion, and intrinsic health simultaneously is another example of prajna. Prajna doesn't divide experience into judgments of being good or bad, acceptable or unacceptable; it simply sees the entire perspective all at once, without polarizing to one side or the other.

My wedding at Green Gulch was an extreme example of an experience of prajna, and it turned out that my foresight was accurate. The marriage was, from traditional standards, impermanent. However, it was due to that marriage I began teaching Karuna Training in Europe. Teaching Karuna Training has always been a personal challenge to fulfill my Buddha activity. Thus the marriage fulfilled its function beautifully, and I remain close to my ex-husband to this day.

The Green Gulch Zen Center and potent garden mandala remain as a place of awakening, a place that's been deeply steeped in Mahayana Buddhism, and we can even imagine the land before it held the Zen Center. Muir Beach, a scenic ocean inlet, has forever been perfect in every way, and all beings who abide there have always encountered many forms of suffering, human and otherwise, through birth, old age, sickness, and death. Prajna discerns the multiple truths of reality and, together with compassion, can hold suffering in equanimity. Seeing "things as they are" is the fruit of the fan and the sword.

Seeing Clearly

There are three aspects to prajna: one is the ability to see clearly, the second is to know what is, and the third is to act directly out of what you see and know. Upaya, or skillful means, occurs when we join clear-seeing, knowing, and acting together with a fully awakened heart of compassion. Mahakaruna is great compassion because it is endowed with discernment, truth-telling, and decisive insights of how to act that arise out of prajna.

We see clearly with prajna because there is no interpreting or holding on to personal points of view; we are unbiased in our ability to see phenomena and, most importantly, others in relationships. The sword symbolizes prajna because we see clearly by cutting through the conceptual mind to the experience of direct perception. Prajna perceives reality directly, without mental conditioning and the biases and obscurations of relative truth. The sword's two-sidedness represents prajna because it cuts attachment to "this" (which is me), and it also cuts attachment to "that" (our projections on others). Prajna is a sharp instrument for seeing "things as they are"— seeing the unbound nature of reality and glimpsing absolute truth.

Fanning the heart's potency is the medicine. However, that is necessary to let go of egoic clinging, which holds on to the concepts of who we are, what we want, and how things should be. We see through these conditioned deceptions of relative truth with prajna, and without maitri toward ourselves, we will experience it too harshly. We may use our insights to make ourselves wrong. When we've established a practice of loving-kindness through our mindfulness-awareness practice, when we see through phenomena to its inherent emptiness, we're seeing-through conditioned perspectives within which we've nested and defended ourselves.

Often, the process of gaining a broader perspective on events in our lives occurs over time and with much introspection and hindsight. We look back at failed relationships or painful circumstances, and in doing so we see all the signs were there from the very beginning. We can get stuck in making ourselves wrong for not seeing what is obvious to us now. Forgiving ourselves and mustering up forgiveness for others often takes time. However, with prajna, clear-seeing occurs on the spot. We see things for what they are while the event is occurring, and we're able to know what is happening and act compassionately with skillful means.

Knowing What Is

The second aspect of prajna that arises directly out of clear-seeing is an intuitive knowing called *discriminating-awareness wisdom*—the ability to discern what is happening in its entirety while understanding the absolute meaning of any given phenomena. We may not be able to hold this type of knowledge in our conceptual minds. But in moments of prajna, when we can go beyond our own projections to a broader perspective, we see glimpses of what is in stark clarity.

The shadows of systemic racism are an excellent example of the capacity to see things systemically and in perspective. When we become aware of this, we don't just see the outer facts of any circumstances, such as lower availability to education and income-earning ventures for Black Americans; we see the underbelly of systemic racism and all the causes and conditions that keep that power-over system in place.

Knowing what is comes with responsibilities; we are inspired to do something about it because we see things clearly and understand what is. Yet we need the third capacity of prajna to know what to do and act directly.

Act Directly

The third aspect of prajna is the result of the first two aspects and allows us to take clear-seeing and intuitive knowledge into embodied skillful means. Skillfulness is necessary for coming to terms with things as they are because once we've exposed ourselves to a kind of wisdom it's like we know too much. If we don't act accordingly it becomes like we are suppressing our wisdom. Again, we need the warmth and heart of compassion to weigh the most compassionate way forward when dealing with the pain and paradoxes life often presents to us.

The compassionate exchange method is straightforward due to the very open and contemplative container we offer to others as compassionate friends. We may not have time in any given moment to set up a full formal container to have a compassionate exchange as we do in Karuna Training; however, we can open our hearts in a flash and exchange ourselves with others in a type of Guerilla Tonglen. We rouse our bodhicitta and remember everyone's intrinsic sanity and feel into the pain that presents itself.

When encountering death or any debilitating diseases or circumstances, in those moments when we have no words and no idea what is helpful to say or do, when our only action is to sit with the discomfort of not knowing and stay connected in the heart—these are moments when it's time to practice Guerilla Tonglen. Guerilla Tonglen is utilizing the breath at the moment and taking on pain of whatever is happening in the room at the moment, staying entirely compassionately present, without a plan or desire to change or fix anything—the skillful means to stay open-hearted in the storm is not knowing.

Paradoxically, knowing what to do is often inspired by the state of not knowing what to do and staying connected in the heart through feeling. Alternating sending and taking on the breath can be grounding for the practitioner at the moment, breathing in the pain of what we are encountering, and breathing out everything good, peaceful, resilient, and wise on the out-breath. This alternation utilizes the oscillating breath to regulate and integrate ourselves in compassion. We remember to practice the embodied action of oscillation, especially when we don't know what to do.

Mahakaruna can exchange with anything entirely through identifying inseparably with the suffering being met. Mahakaruna is a fearless action that requires a significant heart infused with compassion, great compassion. Then bringing the higher knowledge into the mix, we fearlessly raise the sword of prajna to cut our projections on that and ourselves.

For an experiment, the next time you encounter an unsheltered being in the streets or a subway, practice making eye contact and then practice a breath or two of Guerilla Tonglen. The practice of opening our hearts fully and completely and touching into the pain of an unsheltered person allows us to be fearless enough to see, understand fully, and embody our homelessness on the spot. Compassionate Exchange is a tremendous skillful means of joining the fan and the sword to benefit others. Should we open ourselves without the discernment of prajna we can be endangered. Prajna is practical and allows us to work skillfully with circumstances as they are.

CHAPTER XIII

Embracing Not-Knowing Mind

Working as the director of that crisis house in rural California, I had to approach my work with a great deal of *not-knowing mind*, as I was often called on when someone was in an acute mental state. There's a great deal of fear involved when mental stability is being challenged. The ability to truly assist demands that one enters these heightened scenarios with a good dose of equanimity.

One scenario that stays with me is of a man who had locked himself in with his deceased mother's body, and only the stench had alarmed his neighbors enough to call the crisis team. Nobody had seen his mother in years. Her son had cared for her every need, and when she passed, it was too much for him to admit. So he continued with his daily rituals, choosing to ignore the fact that his mother had died. The body was rotting in her bed, but the man continued to attend to her body as if she was alive. It took a few hours to get him to admit that he did know she was no longer living during the crisis call, but he couldn't bear to lose her presence.

Sitting with this man's suffering in Compassionate Exchange took a contemplative presence and a mind of not knowing. Letting go of any agenda, I joined with this man's state of grief and allowed him the time to acknowledge his experience. He was slightly paranoid and distrustful of others when we arrived, yet through exchanging with him, it became apparent he was grieving the death of his mother, his way. Joining with him in Compassionate Exchange was giving him the benefit of the doubt, and through a lot of gaps in conversation, he was able to tell me that without the rituals of caring for his mother, he had no purpose in life. He employed ignorance to deny her passing to remain potent and connected to a purpose.

Bringing a mind of not knowing to Compassionate Exchange is recognizing and touching the truth of human suffering as it is, providing space and bodhichitta, and without necessarily finding a solution. A Contemplative Psychology practitioner's willingness to feel another's pain thoroughly allowed this man to experience his humanness and touch his basic sanity—that sanity of admitting he knew she was gone. People in heightened states notice when others are present, kind, and compassionate, or not.

What makes someone human, approachable, and authentic is the invisible exchange that is easily experienced between two people. Human beings are attuned to exchange, whether we are aware of the phenomena and whether we use it for or against ourselves. Contemplative Psychology requires we trust in a state of mental openness, groundlessness, and space that isn't necessarily comfortable—a state that might leave us feeling vulnerable. Relaxing into a nonreferential space of transparency is the fruition of Contemplative Psychology. With Contemplative Psychology, we offer ourselves to others with authentic presence, an expression of nonjudgmental love, relaxation, and comfort with being vulnerable. We call it a mind of not knowing.

This chapter investigates letting go into this state of not-knowing mind and embracing this innate openness through the practice of

Compassionate Exchange. Embracing a not-knowing mind requires us to develop familiarity with our habitual styles of "knowing." Not-knowing mind also requires a fair amount of *intensity capacity*, discussed in chapter III. Intensity capacity is experienced as a strength of mind to stay present without knowing, even while exchanging with another's suffering. We don't ask why someone is suffering or even who the suffering belongs to because there is no need to find a solution.

Tuning into suffering with a mind of nonjudgmental awareness is one of many forms of offering ourselves in Compassionate Exchange. The ability to resonate with another's feelings through an exchange, without a narrative or the urgency to fix another's problems, is a rare and sought-after experience for those in pain.

We are embracing open moments of space. Relaxation occurs when we adopt a not-knowing mind. Comfort with a not-knowing mind is the fruition of regular meditation practice and familiarizing ourselves with the experience of open non-referential space. There are moments of presence, for example, while walking in nature, when we are in a nonverbal exchange with an animal such as a horse or a dog when we trust the experience of not knowing and openness as a natural state of interaction with others. Attuning to this openness of not knowing is the fruition of Contemplative Psychology.

Not Knowing Requires Intensity Capacity

Life offers us many opportunities to let go of our knowing mind: the unexpected loss of loved ones, the loss of a job or a relationship, a contract falls through, or there is a pandemic and our life gets canceled. In these examples, it's easy to find ourselves standing on the abyss of emptiness, and any suggestion of staying with not knowing is acutely anxiety-provoking. We don't know what's next, and often we don't know who we are because we've defined ourselves by our conditioned existence.

As Americans, culturally, we are trained to define ourselves by what we do in life. In America, specifically, the first question typically asked of a stranger is, "What do you do?" By this we mean *what do you do for livelihood*, or *what do you do with your time to make you a meaningful contributing person to society?* Having lived in Europe for nine years, I noticed the first question typically asked of strangers there is, "Where are you from?" Associating one with a place has more information for Europeans. But in the States, occupation more than location determines stature and class.

In the practice of Compassionate Exchange, we're encouraged to open our hearts without a plan fully. To trust such gaps of unpreparedness, one needs to have already tamed their mind, meaning exercised the mindfulness muscles so the mind will stay with whatever is arising in the present moment, especially when it's emotionally uncomfortable. The ability to experience emotional energy directly without making anything up, suppressing the energy, or dissociating to cope is the practice of not-knowing mind. And the ability to "stay with" whatever energy is arising is intensity capacity.

If we dare to show up as leaders, teachers, or in any kind of authority in life, then we will be asked to answer questions when we do not have the answer. How hard is it for you in a leadership role to say, "I don't know"? I've presented myself as a teacher in Karuna Training and Buddhism for over 25 years, and though I'm experienced, there is so much I don't know. However, I've had the habit of needing to be "in the know." Along the way, I've relaxed with not knowing and actively cultivate a not-knowing mind. I've realized that we always teach what we need to learn ourselves.

I remember teaching Contemplative Psychology in Paris for the first time and discovering that the room was full of ardent psychoanalysts. Psychoanalysis was a form of therapy that was out of vogue in California, where I'd come from, yet very popular in Paris at the time. At the start of the program, I became extremely self-conscious and decided Parisians were intimidating. Then I remembered what I was teaching, and I brought in the notion of maitri, loving-kindness toward myself and others. This helped me to flip my self-conscious mind into a curious mind. I got the group to investigate the ideas I was presenting around Contemplative Psychology and how they translated or not into psychoanalysis. This made my talks into big group discussions, which, I realized, was a much more engaging way to teach everything. More voices are always better than one when it comes to learning, and a teacher's true skill is the ability to tap the wisdom of the greater whole.

Leading with a not-knowing mind is to lead with curiosity and inquiry. When I dare not to know, I automatically sit with openness and curiosity. Being a learner as a teacher is wiser than being a knower. In fact, as a teacher, I've learned to value the mind of not knowing as the most learned capacity teachers can experience.

The Skandhas form our sense of self, or who we fixate on being. Skandhas are the capacities of the mind we group to develop an ego, or how we know we exist. To step into not-knowing mind as a way of life, we are required to become familiar with our habitual ways of knowing.

Knowing and Not Knowing in the Five Families

Letting go of habitual knowing requires we become familiar with our style of creating a false sense of security through "knowing." The Five Buddha Families offer a helpful lens through which to view our habitual tendencies and befriend ourselves as we are. Practicing with the Five Buddha Families evokes familiar energetic and personality styles and allows us to see ourselves and learn to rouse a sense of humor toward our conditioned psychological habits. Our conditioned way of knowing is simply our collection of habits that help us avoid the anxiety-producing experience of not knowing. Of course, we're not the total of our mental practices; they merely serve to express our conditioning and nothing more.

As explained earlier in this book, we examine how our habits of knowing to evolve through the contemplative practice of Maitri Space Awareness (MSA). In MSA practice, one lies in designated postures in the appointed colored rooms and "intensifies" the energies associated with that Buddha family by staying with our relationship to space in the specific posture. The energy of the Buddha families reveals itself in the retreat in relationships and interactions with others. How the energies manifest in each of us is a mystery but has to do with our familial, cultural, and life conditioning. The events in our lives have shaped us and habituated us into the way we are, and then there are the multiple causes and conditions that bring those certain moments to our awareness.

When we're learning about the subtle and sometimes not-so-subtle energies of the Five Buddha Families, we find out we're often the last to know about our energy and its effect on others; these can be things evident to everyone else. For example, I've always been a very energetic person, with more energy than most, and I'm a "get the job done" kind of girl. That maps easily to the Karma Buddha Family, which is about achieving by doing. I never identified as that kind of energetic person in my mind, so I never saw that part of myself before partaking in MSA practice. At the time, however, I was a runner and was doing everything possible to make sure I got in my exercise during the MSA retreat. Doing the Karma Buddha Family posture, that all popped through leaning into that family, which is meant by *intensification* practice. I became manic about running daily. I realized how driven I was around exercise specifically and, in general, the solid conditioned pattern of needing to improve myself through training, through everything. I saw how much Karma energy I possessed, and it shocked me.

Spending time with each of the Buddha families reveals the energetic styles of how people habitually know things, how they approach their lives, and general trends of how people operate in the world. I'm fingerpainting with the Five Buddha Families' energetic styles in the following examples, meaning I'm pointing out tendencies. These examples are not what you *should* experience, and there is no formula, recipe, or "right way" to experience the Buddha family energies. We are each unique in our mental conditioning, and yet we're all familiar with these five energetic patterns, which is why they are called "families," because we are related to these styles in one way or another.

MSA practice supports familiarizing ourselves with emotional and psychological styles to befriend ourselves as we are, instead of changing ourselves into something better. Each of these energetic styles has both wisdom and confusion sides, and multiplicities' manifestations of the Five Buddha energies appear in others. One slogan I've repeated many times in Karuna Training is *the mind that confuses and causes us pain is the same mind that wakes us up!* Unfortunately, there is no trade-in for our minds, at least not yet. Therefore, MSA refines and familiarizes us with our energetic style, which serves us to take responsibility for our energy and its effect on others and supports skillful means in understanding others' nature.

Vajra Buddha Family Knowing

The Vajra Family style is associated with consciousness, or the fifth Skandha. In Vajra, the tendency of "seeing" all angles simultaneously of a situation is essential; knowing all the arguments to any given issue and being mentally astute, logical, and reasonable is all part of the pattern of knowing. Vajra energy is the mental habit of "I see" and therefore "I know." The ability to conceptually figure things out is what knowing is for Vajra Family energy types. Phrases like "I understand the situation clearly," or "Now I see clearly," are indications that the mind is made up and fixed on any given issue. When one's opinion of something has become immovable, then the Vajra Family energy can be a very impenetrable way of knowing.

The way a Vajra energy person discovers "not knowing" is through the practice of inquiry. The ability to open and consider multiple truths of any given situation, numerous ways to see the case is a way for Vajra's energy to unravel the mind's solidity. If you've ever watched a legal television drama, you've seen a well-trained legal mind geared toward understanding the multiple ways to spin reality. When one angle isn't working in a courtroom drama, trained lawyers can pivot on a dime to take the case in another direction.

What is described above is an exaggerated example of how Vajra energy first "sees clearly" and then continues to *look more deeply* for the multiple truths present in every situation. Generally, we look for something, and then we see it as we think it should be. But with a not-knowing mind, we first see something, and then we open and look more deeply. Looking is the act of turning our mind to space and not knowing.

Ratna Buddha Family Knowing

Looking at the habits of knowing in the Ratna Buddha Family's lens assesses reality from feeling, quality, and value. Ratna is associated with the second Skandha capacity of mind, feeling Skandha. Utilizing feeling capacity to exchange with space nonverbally and to sense one's relative safety, status, and worthiness in every situation is what drives knowing from the Ratna perspective. Ratna energy depends on knowing through the currency of vibes, whether one is being accepted, issues of belonging, and evaluating the invisible hierarchies of relationships in all contexts. Whether attending a business meeting, family gathering, or any kind of social event, Ratna energy assesses where one fits into an invisible hierarchy of value. If a host has seated us at a table, we notice our seat has great significance due to people's status at that table. Ratna energy knows by intuiting the quality and worth of ourselves in every given situation.

Not-knowing mind in Ratna is again learning to lead with curiosity and exercise one's sense perceptions to extend further into qualities of every encounter with interest and nonjudgmental awareness. Learning how to feel without evaluation takes mind training in equanimity. Taking the example of where a host has seated you, instead of solidifying the feelings of being dished, one can become curious about who the host has paired them with and why. Through curiosity, we might discover we are sitting at the most exciting and fun table of all.

Padma Buddha Family Knowing

Taking the Padma Buddha Family into habitual ways of knowing lands us in the domain of attachment, perceptions, and reactions. The Padma Family is associated with the Skandha perception impulse, and with Padma Family energy, curiosity is second nature. A Padma energy way of knowing is through confirmation and acceptance. The Padma Buddha Family knows through magnetizing and conquering someone or something into being for or against us. For example, if we've been the star of the evening and feel that everyone likes us, then we know we're okay. Popularity, success, artistic prowess, and connections occupy the knowing of a Padma energy person.

Not knowing in the Padma Family is about tolerating loneliness, being left out, and disconnecting. The wisdom the Padma family imparts is that we are born alone, we live alone (even when we live with others), and we die alone.

Karma Buddha Family Knowing

The Karma Buddha Family is, in many ways, what we in the Northern Hemisphere of America are most familiar with in our habitual way of knowing. Knowing has solid mental concepts of success and achievement. Being successful means we have surpassed others and accomplished something better or more significant than everyone else. It is an active competitive way of knowing. Karma Buddha energy dominates many fields of livelihood—skill-based accomplishments, such as those found in sports, academics, and the entertainment industry, where competition is driving success.

Not knowing in the Karma family requires us to compare our accomplishments with others and befriend ourselves as we are. Karma energy learns to trust not knowing through curiosity and inquiry, like every other family. Here the comparative aspect of mind is utilized to question what we do not know personally and as a species and to compile that information and build a better widget or come up with a better solution.

Buddha Buddha Family Knowing

The final and most challenging to negotiate element in knowing and not knowing is in the Buddha Buddha family, which hosts a trepidatious border between resting in not knowing and slipping into ignorance. Spacing out and not caring is how Buddha Family handles knowing. Buddha Family energy employs space to ignore what they don't know and to actively not care whether they know or not. For example, the painful relationships we might have in our family, we develop habits of not thinking about those people if we can help it. We simply avoid the sore points and know that that is not where we want to go with our energy or attention.

Resting in not knowing the mind is not the same as forgetting or ignoring something; it's remaining actively awake, present, and connected while not fixing our minds on any opinions or diagnosis about someone's status in life. Ignoring is not the same as not knowing. Not knowing in Buddha is being fully present, awake, and curious, but not forgetting the situation; therefore, not ignoring the complete picture of another requires staying open and not being preoccupied with ourselves.

Working with What Is Emerging

Becoming familiar with our conditioned ways of knowing supports a depth of information in almost all situations. A not-knowing mind is what prepares us for working with what is emerging on the spot. To be available to work with what is emerging requires we get out of the way. Compassionate Exchange work may appear simple and intuitive at the onset, but for most of us, we often join into conversations with clouded minds, full of thinking about ourselves mostly. Shunryu Suzuki, the great Zen Master, says, "When you study Buddhism, you should have a general house cleaning of your mind."[47]

Working with Compassionate Exchange compels us to free ourselves from our conditioned preconceived ideas. Familiarizing ourselves with ourselves takes time to be with ourselves and study our habits of mind with loving-kindness and patience. First, we begin on the meditation cushion, and that need for space and time with ourselves continues as we start to offer ourselves in Compassionate Exchange, to be free enough to work with what is emerging.

---

47 Shunryu, Suzuki, *Zen Mind Beginner's Mind* (New York & Tokyo: Weatherhill, 1970), p. 110.

CHAPTER XIV

The Intimacy of
"Not One, Not Two"

F eeling comfortable and leading with not knowing requires
strength of mind, meaning that we experience so much
awareness that we notice the mere presence of a mote of dust in
the air. Like the perk of a deer's ears in the forest at the sound of a
distant crunch of a footstep, or the ability to detect the first waft of
fall in the air, we can develop a nuanced perception. For example,
we can see, hear, smell, taste, and touch space—or the lack of space
in the present moment.

Fully present mind-body awareness evokes an intimacy with the
world that is sometimes frightening when it occurs suddenly or
unexpectedly. People tell of clear perception they experienced amid
an accident or an unexpected traumatic event as if time were moving
in slow motion. To this day, I remember the feeling of the ground
rolling under my desk during the 1989 Loma Prieta earthquake in
San Francisco. I was tidying up and preparing to leave work after
a long day of therapy sessions. Suddenly, the receptionist screamed
"earthquake!" and rushed to brace herself between the door frame

of my office. I distinctly remember seeing and feeling the running track outside my office window undulating like a wave. That motion is still rippling in my body in the retelling of the event.

These moments are often fraught with anxiety. However, when the mind has been processed with mindfulness-awareness, there is much more preparation for sudden experiences of discontinuity. In Buddhism, first, the mind is tamed with the practice of mindfulness-awareness and then subsequently trained, meaning the muscle of awareness is strengthened to stay present when reference points disappear. Training the mind allows for concepts of time and space to loosen and eventually expand. With steady meditation practice, we find out it's possible to taste and stabilize one's mind from the blinding grip of the Skandhas and one's past mental conditioning.

In this chapter, the experience of *emptiness* is investigated, and we explore the fruition of Contemplative Psychology, transmuting confusion into wisdom in working with difficult emotions. In Sanskrit, emptiness is referred to as *shunyata*. "Emptiness" could be the problematic word. It often carries the nihilistic implication of clamping down on or denying experience. A more accurate translation of shunyata would be "unbound openness."[48]

Brilliant Sanity

Through recognizing and attuning to this "unbound openness," one evolves one's intrinsic sanity into *brilliant sanity*. As explained by the

---

48 Lief, Judith, "Shunyata & Linguistics I" from *Speaking of Silence: Christian and Buddhists in Dialogue* (Halifax: Vajradhatu Publications, 2005), compiled and edited by Susan Szpakowski, p. 136.

Board of Editors for the *Naropa Institute Journal of Psychology*, the emblem "brilliant sanity" proclaims the existence of inherent wakefulness that can be pointed to, recognized, and encouraged through psychological work. This is not metaphysics or metapsychology, nor is it some idealized picture. It is genuine experience that is simple, direct, and sane. It arises from clarifying the nature of mind processes."[49]

Brilliant sanity is a mind free of ego, free from the mental conditioning of our past, which momentarily liberates one from the Skandha activity. In these micro-moments of openness, all one's sense faculties are acutely aware; in fact, our focus is razor-sharp, and sense perceptions are discerned as "not one, not two."[50]

"Not one, not two" is a slogan made famous by Zen teacher Shunryu Suzuki Roshi and requires contemplation. It's common to hear the phrase "we are all one," especially in esoteric and spiritual circles. From a Buddhist perspective, however, there is still an identity in statements such as "we are all one." This statement references an ego of togetherness and connotes we are not alone. In fact, we are alone, and our togetherness does not make us all one when discussing emptiness, or egolessness. In the shunyata state, we're not anything that can be referenced or identified.

At the same time, we're not two, either. It's automatic to live life as if every being and experience is separate from everything else, while, in fact, we are continually interdependent with everyone and everything else in the world. Thus, we're not two.

---

49 The Board of Editors, *Naropa Institute Journal of Psychology*, Volume 1, No. 1 (January 1980): p. 1.

50 Suzuki, Shunryu, *Zen Mind Beginner's Mind* (New York & Tokyo: Weatherhill, 1970), p. 25.

Brilliant sanity is realized when we dare to face our experience of "not one, not two" directly by feeling the conditioned nature of mental habits, the quality and natural space of emotions as they're arising. In Contemplative Psychology, we process our minds and work directly with the energy of emotions so that our intrinsic sanity is processed into the shining jewel living within us all. In those moments of offering ourselves to others and the world with loving-kindness, compassion, joy, and equanimity, we're able to embody and manifest our brilliant sanity.

Intensification Practice

In Contemplative Psychology, experiencing and integrating "not one, not two" is how we uncover our brilliant sanity with which we are all endowed. Having a tamed and trained mind to meet the moment with complete openness and to stay present in the face of confusion, groundlessness, and suffering is the fruition of Contemplative Psychology.

Usually, one gains insight through glimpses of emptiness before any realization of shunyata is afforded. By studying the mind's capacities, which are bound together in Skandha activity, habits of reaction, and suppression of a mind that is busy affirming that we do indeed exist, we find out that the busyness of the mind is distracting and making us miss out on the magic of life's energies. As Chögyam Trungpa says, "There are several stages in relating with energy and emotions: seeing, hearing, smelling, tasting, touching, and transmuting."[51] In Contemplative Psychology, the work is to become familiar with the energy through sense perceptions, embracing inner sensations, the

---

51 Trungpa, Chögyam, "Chaos as Opportunity" in "The Lion's Roar" from *The Collected Works of Chögyam Trungpa, Volume 2* (Boston & London: Shambhala, 2003), p. 509.

discomfort of emotions, and eventually moving on to transmuting emotions, which occurs once we are stable enough in our minds to be fully present to energy as it is arising, both in ourselves as well as in others.

Through contemplative methods, specifically *intensification practice* utilized in Maitri Space Awareness, we discover that the same capacities of mind that trap us are the same capacities of mind that also liberate us. We can medicate and intoxicate the mind, which helps to suppress emotions. In the end, those numbing behaviors and substances become addictive. To realize and work directly with the energy of the mind, one learns to work with whatever state the mind is found in the present moment, without self-medicating or suppressing the energy.

Utilizing the Four-Step Practice, discussed in chapter VII, is learning how to approach emotional energy with loving-kindness and nonjudgmental awareness, even when our mind feels confused and unmanageable.

Chögyam Trungpa introduced intensification practice through MSA, proscribing staying with and leaning into emotional energy and space. When we work with energy through intensification practice, the energy is dynamic, and sometimes it "bloats and pops," meaning the energy is heightened so that one's awareness shifts instantly and dramatically. One suddenly perceives and experiences reality completely differently than a moment before, with a more open and spacious perception. Intensification is practiced in MSA retreat settings where we have the time and hopefully safety to explore space through the nuanced awareness of the mind. Through this form of study, one becomes familiar with specific styles of energy and can begin to trust in one's natural openness rather than the conditioned ways we habitually confirm that we exist.

One example of how "bloat and pop" occurs happened to me during my first MSA retreat. I was 24 years old and living with my boyfriend during the three-month MSA retreat at Shambhala Mountain Center (then Rocky Mountain Dharma Center). My boyfriend was notoriously flirtatious and not particularly committed to me during the program. I experienced a lot of paranoia and fear in that relationship; jealousy was the primary emotion I was ensconced in, which relates to the Karma Buddha Family. While intensifying the Karma Family, my jealousy became very heightened, so much so that while intensifying the Karma Family posture, I decided my boyfriend must be cheating on me. He knew I was occupied in that hour, and in a confused state of mind, I concocted that it would be a perfect time to catch him in the act of cheating on me. I left the Karma Family room and began crawling through the rough mountain sagebrush on my knees to sneak up on him in the trailer we were sharing. Suddenly, he came up behind me and shouted, "What are you doing?" My mind instantly popped, and I began to cry and laugh simultaneously at the absurdity of my jealous actions. The romantic aspect of that relationship was over shortly after that incident, for everyone's basic sanity!

In undertaking intensification practice, one invokes faith in intrinsic health by leaning into emotional energy with presence and loving-kindness. By doing so, the wisdom reveals itself, or not. Intensification, remember, is a third step in working skillfully with energy, after taming the mind. Vajrayana Buddhism respects and incorporates other means of working with a fixated mind as well.

Transmuting Confusion into Wisdom

Once the mind is trained to rouse loving-kindness, one must study the wisdom of Mandala of the Five Buddha Families, along with the confusion element of the families. Recall the mind map of Contemplative Psychology and the formation of the ego. Each of the Five Buddha Families is connected to one of the Skandhas. As a result, each of the Buddha families has a confused egoic tendency and an ego wound, an emotional direction the respective emotions tend toward when activated.

Each of the Buddha families maps to a complex emotional inter-action and each family is associated with a Skandha, or capacity of mind used to build ego. Each of the Five Buddha Families has correlated wisdom, too, in which to transmute the confusion. How the wisdom shows up is individual, contextual, and specific to the person experiencing the emotion. I am fingerpainting again with the energies to give examples of how each disturbing emotion might transmute into wisdom.

Intensification methods are unique to Vajrayana Buddhism, which teaches the energetic correlation between confusion and wisdom, or insanity and sanity. Confused solidified emotions and the wisdom counterpart both arise from the same capacities of mind. These capacities of mind relate to the Five Skandhas and the Five Buddha Families simultaneously, and there are correlated capacities of mind driving one's confusion and/or wisdom. On the one hand, we can manifest a solidified egoic stance to prove that we exist in one Buddha family style. On the other hand, we can recognize "not one, not two" and be freed to manifest the associated wisdom of that Buddha family.

	Buddha Family Skandha[52] Function	Ego Wound	Wisdom
Buddha / Form "First split"	Ignoring the open, fluid, and intelligent quality of space. Fear of space, identifying with separateness. Self-observing ignorance.	I am cut off	**All-Encompassing Space** An awake state, with engaged sense perceptions and capacity to hold everything in equanimity, without accepting or rejecting.
Ratna / Feeling	Weaving the imaginary fabric of feeling for safety, caution, or neutrality. This preverbal state of mind feels "me" to be real and struggles to maintain and enhance a sense of solid self. Experience threatens to reveal our transitoriness. Feeling Skandha is the basis of exchange.	I am unworthy	**Equanimity** The capacity of the mind to rest in nonjudgmental awareness without any feeling of reaction toward or against, in a discriminating open space.
Padma / Perception "perception/impulse"	Engaging sense-perceptions with concepts of "liking" and "not liking" or feeling neutral with an attitude of "couldn't care less." This fickle state of mind makes things up, projects them on space, and then reacts to one's projections.	I am unlovable	**Discriminating Awareness** The discerning capacity of mind that sees phenomena through space, distinctly and accurately knowing what to accept and what to reject.

52 Ego—a transitory, discontinuous event that, in our confusion, appears to be quite solid and continuous.
Ego wound—tendency of self-involvement.
Skandhas— a Sanskrit word meaning 'heaps of experiences' which is the makeup of ego. The five Skandhas are movements of mind, that conglomerate to form the illusion of existence, or ego hood.

Karma	Formation "intelligence"	51 Samskaras (mental formations) penetrate the subconscious as habitual mental patterns that project the 6 Realms. Absorbed in the idea of a solid, continuous sense of who "I am" *and* a solid, continuous projection of who "you are"—we freeze patterns of relationship with paranoia, panic, craving, and mistrust, which fortifies projected fears.	I am powerless	**All-Accomplishing Action** The ability to know what to do in context and apply the appropriate action of pacifying, enriching, magnetizing, or destroying.
Vajra	Consciousness	8 Consciousnesses (Described as part of the fifth Skandha in chapter II) are the mechanisms by which we utilize our seeds from past events and make them reference our story and bring continuity to who we think we are. There are many paradoxes skipped over in this process, leaving gaps for the wisdom to shine through.	I am unforgivable	**Mirror-Like** The capacity to reflect all aspects of any given phenomenon, with a corresponding understanding of conflicting and paradoxical arguments.

Navigating out of the confused state of mind toward the innate wisdom of emotions is a process called *transmutation*, which simply means changing from one state of mind to another instantly. In the application of MSA and intensification practice, however, transmutation is much more connected to the notion of "bloat and pop." Liberating our confusion by staying with the energy of emotions as they are. Eventually, the energy opens, mental conditioning falls away, and the power and wisdom of the energy is what's left. We can't conceptualize our way into wisdom; wisdom is revealed through the natural state of shunyata.

As Chögyam Trungpa says, "Transmutation . . . does not reject the basic quality of emotions, but it's like the alchemical process of turning lead to gold."[53] Approaching our emotions with the intention of opening to them in their natural state assumes an already contemplatively trained mind. Otherwise, it would feel like we were asking you to stand in a thunderstorm with an electrical antenna extended.

Buddha Ignorance Transmutes into All-Encompassing Space

In the mandala center, the Buddha Buddha Family is associated with the element space and the first Skandha "form," or first split. It is the point at which the mind divides space into "this" and "that," or me and you. The solidified emotion is ignorance, and the element is space. In the Buddha Family, the element of space is employed to suppress, block, and ignore emotional energy, or anything creating discomfort and confusion. Buddha Family tendency is to be spaced out, neglectful, missing the nuance of awareness, and often missing what is in front of one's nose.

The wisdom of Buddha is *all-encompassing space*, which is open awareness that stays present through holding complete cognizance.

---

53 Trungpa, Chögyam, "Chaos as Opportunity" in "The Lion's Roar" from *The Collected Works of Chögyam Trungpa, Volume 2* (Boston & London: Shambhala, 2003), p. 510.

Buddha Family's ignorance is difficult to discern for oneself; we don't know what we don't know. When the mind is no longer employing space to split off from others and stay connected to the present inseparability, discomfort, and claustrophobia of self-consciousness, then the Buddha Family's wisdom of accommodation is born. Like the Buddha, there is no reaction completely spacious, awake, and able to comprehend without reaction whatsoever.

We can discern an awakening from ignorance once we've woken up to anything we've been ignoring. A good example is how our collective societal ignorance is currently in discussion on systemic racism. It is easy for white people to ignore the lived experience of people of color, specifically Black Americans. Once we begin to open to the pain of what is being displayed and connect through compassion to the suffering caused by our ignorance, the ignorance transmutes into an eye-opening accommodating space of what is in front of us; in other words, we make room for the painful conversation and further realization of what we don't know.

Ratna Pride Transmutes into the Wisdom of Equanimity

In the southern direction of the Mandala, the Ratna Buddha Family is associated with the second Skandha, feeling. There is a preverbal capacity in each of us to feel into whether any given situation is safe, unsafe, or neutral. For some, this capacity is more exercised than others in that early childhood or developmental trauma can make this capacity extremely sensitized. We are in the domain of quality and subliminal feeling. Ratna's challenging emotion is pride, whose flip side is always poverty. Worthiness is an issue in the Ratna Family and measuring one's worth in relation to others is the preoccupation of the mind.

The wisdom of Ratna is equanimity, which is the ability not to react, judge, project onto circumstances, or hold on to either accepting or rejecting phenomena. Equanimity is essential when working with difficult emotions in any case. And we can understand the experience of equanimity is finding the middle point between poverty, feeling less than, or pride, from "better than" feelings. There is a medium point of balance in exercising an unbiased mind, where judgment suspends toward ourselves and others. Everything is regarded as "just information."

Transmuting pride or poverty to equanimity is dependent on genuinely making friends with ourselves, opening our hearts to others, and rousing compassion for those who are suffering. When caught in the brutal self-critique of feeling unworthy, one struggles to open to a bigger perspective, like the suffering of another. Developing equanimity through rousing maitri (loving-kindness) involves the generosity of raising our gaze to allow in the rest of the world. I remember someone giving me the feedback when I was in my twenties that it felt like I didn't care for others because I was too occupied with myself. It was both shocking and compassionate feedback, although I don't remember liking it at the time. In retrospect, it took making friends with myself and valuing myself enough to relax, and then the world comes to you. The wisdom of equanimity is holding an extensive and open perspective with no self-preoccupation whatsoever.

Padma Passion Transmutes into Discriminating Awareness Wisdom

In the western domain of the Padma Family, we are working with the third Skandha, perception, or perception/impulse as Chögyam Trungpa described it. The Padma Buddha Family is associated with the struggles of passion and blinding desire. Where being loved, accepted, and appreciated becomes a dependency, and whatever object is fixated on is only temporary and in the service of being confirmed.

The wisdom of Padma is discriminating awareness wisdom, otherwise known as prajna—the ability to discern and see through self-serving desires. Prajna sees unbound openness and allows the space of the heart to connect to the suffering of others. Thus, prajna is necessary for the actual development of compassion.

Thus, the struggles of passion transmute into compassion through the ability to endure the loneliness of human existence. One example is when we realize that nobody can make us happy or feel fully fulfilled, completely loved, and seen. Placing that burden of expectation on another is bound for disaster; when one has the prajna to see through one's self-delusion, then the heart and the mind widen enough to see and feel beyond one's self-serving concerns. When the endless tail-chasing after being loved is seen through for what it is, that is when passion transmutes into discriminating awareness wisdom.

Karma Envy Transmutes into the Wisdom of All Accomplishing Action

In the northern domain of the mandala, the Karma Buddha Family is associated with envy or jealousy and the mind is consumed with one-upmanship and the advancement of self. The Karma Family is complex with layers of comparison, one against the other, jockeying for a seat of being the best, most accomplished, and most influential one can be. This vibrant energy is dominant in many current professions, like academia, the entertainment industry, and even spiritual teachers and the New Age, wherever it feels the stakes are high and much is at risk.

The Karma wisdom is counter-intuitively All-Accomplishing Action, meaning there's a potentially skillful component that emerges from a comparative mind. Let's consider ingenuity and the advancements in technology. A comparative capacity of the mind is necessary to build a better widget. One must be discerning of what has happened before and make it better. Accomplishment does not have to dominate others or aggrandize oneself, even though we often see the contrary of this everywhere we look.

Vajra Anger Transmutes into Mirror-Like Wisdom

Finally, in the eastern domain of the mandala, the Vajra Buddha Family is associated with the fifth Skandha, consciousness. The Vajra family is related to the emotion of anger. Anger is constantly fueled by justification or the need to be right. Just consider when we find ourselves in a disagreement with someone, and notice how many times we run the argument over and over in our heads to justify why we're right and the other is wrong!

The wisdom of the Vajra Family is mirror-like wisdom, which takes that same tendency of mind, bringing justification in all its myriad reflections conscious, without the need to be right. The unbound openness of mind allows for there to be many perspectives of consciousness for any given situation. Mirror-like wisdom is clear-seeing. Mirror-like wisdom is like it sounds, the capacity of a still lake to reflect exactly its environment and circumstances as they are.

In all incidents of transmuting a confused mind into a wisdom mind, all five wisdom components of the mind are present. We divide and study the Five Buddha Families to be nuanced and intimate with energy and the capacities of the mind. The ability to accommodate all emotional energies, hold the energy with equanimity, discern the complete picture of what is transpiring, act accordingly with skill, and see all sides of any story clearly is the drawing of all wisdom. The transmutation of confusion to wisdom utilizes all wisdom capacities of the mind to wake up to things as they are.

As Chögyam Trungpa explains, "Transmutation takes place with the understanding of shunyata and then the sudden discovery of energy. You realize that you no longer have to abandon anything. You begin to see the underlying qualities of wisdom in your life situation, which means that there is some kind of leap. If you are highly involved in one emotion such as anger, then by having a sudden glimpse of openness, which is shunyata, you begin to see that you do not have to suppress your energy. You do not have to keep calm and suppress the energy of anger, but you can transform your aggression into dynamic energy. It is a question of how open you are, how much you are willing to do it. If there is less fascination and satisfaction with the explosion and release of your energy, then there is more likelihood of transmuting it. Once we become involved with the fascination and satisfaction of energy, then we are unable to transmute it."[54]

---

54 Trungpa, Chögyam, "Tantra" in "Cutting through Spiritual Materialism" from *The Collected Works of Chögyam Trungpa, Volume 3* (Boston & London: Shambhala, 2003), p. 173.

SECTION FOUR

The Moment-to-Moment Art of Compassionate Exchange

CHAPTER XV

Love and All the Elements

Section four is dedicated to how to apply Contemplative Psychology in one's everyday life. How to take the magic of leaning into the Five Buddha Family Mandala and bring an endowed and vitalized ritual awareness into our daily lives. We also explore the travails of living in a time of impending ecological catastrophe, along with the natural embracing of death and the contemplative journey of the bardos[55] in everyday life. These chapters illuminate Contemplative Psychology in action and support the deepening of Compassionate Exchange with our world.

Imagine standing in a circle in an open field, in the shadow of large cottonwood trees in a high dessert pine forest in Southern California. The Tehachapi Range is way too dry for mid-June, and the air is stringent. We are all challenged in the hot, dry canyon air of a Tibetan Buddhist retreat center. The center has generously opened its doors to Karuna Training, in the slim pickings of finding a post-pandemic seminar house. Karuna Training is regarded

---

55 Bardo—a Tibetan Buddhist word that defines the transitional space between death and rebirth.

as a close relative in this Tibetan tradition, inspired by the work of Chögyam Trungpa, who is renowned among all traditions of Tibetan Buddhism.

The Mandala of the Five Buddha Families is being evoked in sacred ritual, however, in the most ecumenical way possible. The mandala is being constructed in the lowest part of the land close to a creek, on a wood-chipped spot in the forest. The students find natural objects to create the mandala circle, using rocks, sticks, and pinecones to construct the boundaries of both the outer and inner mandala. The Buddha Buddha Family is in the center because it is space, and every other element arises out of space and dissolves back into space.

The mandala is being constructed as a teaching and an empowerment tool, training participants in how to evoke the elemental energies of the Five Buddha Families. The elements include Buddha—space, Vajra—water, Ratna—earth, Padma—fire, and Karma—wind family element.

Participants at this first deepening week are instructed on the core phases of evoking sacred mandalas, meaning using one's own voice to participate in the morning ritual of constructing and evoking the element of the day at the mandala.

Evoking love for all the elements is a shamanic way to find voice and commune with the unseen forces of the world. Contemplative Psychology understands that reality is living, co-evolving, and co-arising out of the moment-to-moment choices of how we conduct ourselves in our body, speech, and mind, and with one another. Our choices, reactions, and simple words impact other aspects of life on the planet and in the universe. How we exchange with the natural world and beyond actually matters and has consequences. Nothing is predestined but, instead, all is unfolding in the present moment out of numerous causes and conditions co-ripening. Understanding and integrating our interconnected nature to the elements helps us to recognize that it does matter how we conduct ourselves and that basic respect and gratitude for the elements do matter.

Studying and communing with the five elements in the context of the Five Buddha Family Mandala heightens our sense of interconnectedness with the most primordial and living aspect of our worlds. In Karuna Training, we highlight how to access these sacred everyday elements directly, and practice standing firm in our capacity to speak to our personal relationship to this kind of everyday sacredness.

As a society, we've delegated our voice and capacity to commune with the sacred to those in power, whoever that is for us culturally; people such as priests, rinpoches, and therapists are considered designated conduits to the sacred. We seem to think of them as the ones who are more capable than ourselves to be a conduit to cosmic wisdom.

What is your experience, as we explore this capacity to commune with the energies we are made from—in fact, the entire world is made from?

The Fruit of Sacred Ritual

Through contemplative methods, one discovers the most outer aspect of the Five Buddha Family Mandala. The true form of the mandala is the five elements. The outer aspect is the body of the mandala, and through sacred ritual, we practice evoking the intrinsic health of the elements by singing their praises and expressing gratitude for their omnipresence. As we do this, the elemental magic of the world reveals itself, or not.

We study the Five Buddha Families to be more refined in our experience of awareness of emotional energy, but we begin with the elemental nature of the Five Buddha Families. We start with the elements because it's hard to blame an element for performing as it does. For example, the oxygen we breathe may be polluted, but we don't fault the air for that. Or a fire might burn down our house, but usually, we don't criticize the fire for the destruction. When we study the outer elemental nature of the Five Buddha Families, we begin to see how these five elements are the makeup of our world, mirror back our emotional experience, and comprise the texture of our minds.

Rituals are essential for the individual to belong because rituals create a community in the sacred dimensions of reality. Otherwise, we ignore the sacred dimensions or take this aspect of reality for granted. Therefore, there needs to be some sense of ceremony and community as a witness to mark our relationship with the sacred.

In Karuna Training, we present ritual in an ecumenical evocation of the form of the Five Buddha Families, which helps people make contact in as genuine a way as possible. We often feel contrived when we speak out in sacred rituals, especially when we don't have a script or a prescribed chant prewritten. As modern humans, we have been untrained in knowing how to connect heaven and earth in our bodies, speech, and mind. Having a voice in sacred rituals is something we have known as humans from before we can remember. Indigenous cultures the world over know how to enact a sacred ritual in the community, and the health of their communities thrive on these ceremonies.

Before I moved to Europe to teach Contemplative Psychology, I was the program director of a small eating disorder unit in a hospital in

Concord, California. For me, this unit was job number four in a series of five eating disorder units I worked in from the early '80s through the early '90s. However, I held this position while I was studying anthropology and ritual at the California Institute of Integral Studies to pursue a doctorate.

I had already had a crisis of faith in the entire field of psychology and was seeking an exit from the psychological paradigm at the time. I had switched my major in grad school from East-West Psychology to Psychological Anthropology in order to get a wider lens on the issue of women, ritual, and food. This small eating disorder program was doing poorly financially as the recipient of a general fiscal tightening up in hospital environments. I was under management pressure to put heads in beds and keep revenue up, but by then, I had very little faith in the paradigm of in-patient eating disorder treatment.

I decided to throw caution to the wind and turned this 28-day program for eating disorders into a four-week program on reclaiming our bodies, speech, and mind through sacred rituals. I aimed to transmit the inseparability of confusion and wisdom, and eating disorders are always enacted ritually, meaning the behavior is repetitive. I took that repetitive behavior as a sign of intrinsic health and sought a more uplifted replacement to disordered ritual, with sacred ritual. I had the notion then that the mind that confuses us is the same mind that wakes us up.

Drawing heavily from my training in Contemplative Psychology and the Five Buddha Family Mandala, we studied different Buddha family energies each week. The young clients explored these Buddha family energies very personally. Learning to relate to space through meditation was key to the pedagogy, accompanied by a deep dive into one Buddha family energy. For example, on the Ratna Family, we took up the issue of earth, sustenance, generosity, balance, pride, and poverty; we explored the concept of the hungry ghost, which was all too familiar for the bulimic client. A hungry ghost is an image from Tibetan Buddhist iconography of a creature with a large belly and a very small mouth, a being with insatiable hunger. No matter what, that hunger cannot be satiated. We also studied the flip side of poverty—generosity—and being less judgmental of ourselves. On Fridays, we took a group outing and practiced self-designed sacred rituals outdoors. On Earth Day, we went to the redwood forest and hugged trees, on Water Day we went to the ocean and offered up symbols of that which we wanted to purify, and on Fire Day we sat on a mountaintop and burned sage and juniper and made prayers of forgiveness.

The young women in the clinic responded overwhelmingly positively to sacred rituals and these contemplative practices. Some of them reported how well they felt doing these practices to their psychiatrists. Near the end of that program, the physician's group called me into the medical council, and they questioned me on my "alternative" methods. I told them I was teaching girls with eating disorders a different approach to ritual, a different way to bind themselves to the world through appreciation instead of self-consciousness. The physicians' wish to pathologize our clients was another nail in the coffin of my trust in the paradigm of psychotherapy.

Don't get me wrong, I know there is a place in society today for therapy. I would argue that we have ended up with this need due to our isolation from community and ritual. I have been teaching on the need for sacred and mundane rituals for many years, and mundane rituals most importantly are about bringing mindfulness to the repetitive actions we practice daily to bind ourselves to our world. The mundane rituals we do with our phones, with our bodies, with our speech, with loved ones, coworkers, and with our emotions. How do we ritually treat ourselves on a moment-to-moment basis?

I also challenge the notion that addiction is pathological. Addiction is destructive, but it originates simply with seeking connection, which we all do with all kinds of means, things, and people, daily. Seeing addictions as a desire for connection allows for the possibility of transmuting addiction into a ritual of love, which evokes intrinsic health and kindness.

I will take the Five Buddha Family Mandala as a template and introduce the tenets of sacred ritual with each step of the mandala and its elemental wisdom.

The Accommodation and Boundaries of Space

Ironically, we need to boundary space to experience space. To experience space, we need a form, one of the many paradoxical truths in learning the inseparability of confusion and wisdom. All the while, when we boundary the space to create a mandala, we make space.

The first form we learn in Contemplative Psychology is a meditation practice, which is a way to experience space. We need to anchor in form, our breath, as we learn to rest our mind in its natural openness, which is space. The same is true in sacred rituals; we need to create a boundaried form to anchor in the space of our intention.

We stand in a circle in space; within and without, the thickest element in the universe is space! Yet we can't feel space; we merely feel the textures of space, which are the other elements: heat (fire), wind (air), support (earth), and humidity (water). And when we are still enough, we're invited further into the potent presence of space. Thus, space must be discovered through presence and silence.

Space feels limitless, like staring deep into a cloudless blue sky. When we consider space, we realize everything arises out of space, exists in space, and returns to space. The best we can do is have a glimpse of awareness of the passing of things in space. The element of space manifests as present awareness.

Space is experienced when we touch the absence of tension, struggle, and aggression and momentarily can accommodate everything without effort, stress, or commentary. We're open to anything, fresh, clear-seeing, and unconstrained. We accept what is present and touch it with an all-accommodating openness of the present moment. In this way, space is eternally available. Feel how space invites awareness to shine.

Space can also be engulfing, dismissive, blunt, and massively thick. We have learned to employ space when we fall into the depth of sloth, stupor, and ignorance. With the density of enlisting space, we oppress others with our deadened aloofness and lack of awareness. Ignoring is how we get lost in space, and this can be habit-forming.

When we evoke space in sacred ritual, we call space to our bodies to be permeable and awake; we call space to our speech to be nonbiased and rest when we are at pause, and we call space to our minds in unconditional non-self-conscious awareness. So, call space and set the boundaries of your mandala.

The Reflective Prism of Water: Making Praise and Offerings

In sacred rituals, we make elemental offerings in form and voice, singing praise and expressing selflessness. Water, the most precious element in accomplishing sacred praise, glistens and flows with appreciation and clear-seeing. As we reflect on the nature of water, in its many containers—a lake, the ocean, the rain, the river, a vessel, or our bodies—we focus on how dominant water is in our lives and give thanks.

We reflect on how we take water for granted when it flows from the tap, in the shower, to what we drink, in our blood, and our bodies. Think about water's qualities and consider its qualities: fresh, cleansing, cooling, fluid, reflective, and transparent. Sometimes the water is unknown, such as the ocean's depths, and water's potency can slowly wear away an entire mountain range.

Water is a long-standing metaphor for the multiplicities of quality in our minds. Water and its many manifestations are an excellent measure for the speed and fluidity of one's mind. On the meditation cushion, we can tune into the mirror of the mind and reflect on the nature of our state of mind using a water metaphor. Sometimes our thoughts are a gushing Colorado waterfall in spring. Sometimes our thoughts are a trickling brook, barely there but enough for a tadpole to emerge. Sometimes our minds are frozen shut, and we feel we cannot get close to ourselves. Sometimes we're in a boiling rage over an off-handed comment, which remains with us and we can't cool down. All these metaphors of waters are a way to feel the mind and its quality of movement.

Water also has an aggressive side and requires respect. Water can be destructive and takes on the temperature in its container. When we evoke water as our teacher, we can reflect on the attributes of this vital resource and make offerings to the miracle of water!

The Generosity and Aspirations of the Earth Element

The earth element is infinitely generous; just think about the atrocities we humans have practiced on the earth with our mining, exploding, wars, drilling, and polluting, and yet the earth will prevail! We as a species may not, but the earth will continue to evolve and house its inhabitants without rent or complaint. Thus, in sacred ritual, the earth is good to express gratitude toward and ask for that which mind desires. The earth is the ultimate vessel of generosity.

Consider how the earth manifests in nature: through soil that feeds and nourishes us, through peaks, rocks, sand, marble, plants, vegetables, and flowers, fresh meadows and snow-covered mountains—the planet Earth is a cornucopia of experiential wonder. Then there is what we can make from the earth to consume, travel, barter, control, and codify. The earth can be solid, fertile, rich, barren, green, hollow, and overpoweringly beautiful. And the earth manifests the constant display of life and death simultaneously, in decay providing ground for new life.

Earth is also devouring and can manifest as unstable, like in an earthquake. Or earth can be arid, harsh, and lifeless like in a desert. It is the source of richness and poverty, the spark of pride, and a painful reminder of lack. Therefore, in sacred ritual, the earth element, in all its generosity, is the perfect place in the mandala to make a request. It's hard for some humans to ask for what they want, and when doing so, we're often unrealistic and concrete about the outcome. That is why we can learn to use earth as inspiration and make aspirations from a place of abundance and wealth. We know to aspire from the place of a rich and generous heart.

How do you appreciate the earth element in your life? Do you experience too much earth? Are you lacking earth? Invite earth into your experience and make an aspiration that includes the bounty of the earth and the ability to receive and be nourished in our bodies.

The Celebration and Dangerous Magnetism of Fire

The fire element is omnipresent through the sun, the stars, the moon, and the warmth of our bodies. Fire has the capacity to create, to invite growth, and, simultaneously, consume and devour everything with which it comes in contact. Fire purifies and transmutes our confusion into joy, our desire into compassion, and, therefore, fire is the most appropriate element to allow things to ripen and mature.

Fire can be dangerous and sacrosanct as well, meaning not something to mess with. Often in my rituals in Karuna, since they often take place in the west and in the arid countryside, we do not invite fire as a teacher out of respect, but we do celebrate the connectivity of fire's nature.

In sacred ritual there is always a point when the boundaries have been set, praises and offerings have been made, and aspiration has been made toward whatever is being celebrated. Then comes the point where the community must rouse one collective voice in celebration and feast. This is part of every sacred ritual, the ecstatic expression of love, appreciation, joy, connectivity, our purpose, and our sacred impermanence.

Fire element reflects the aspect of ourselves as humans that is seeking connection and warmth, love and affection, belonging and togetherness. When we are cut off from this communal aspect, we are lost and isolated as human beings. The rise of mental illness in the landscape of humanity is partially due to living in such isolated circumstances when we need each other. We live in our own houses, and when privileged, we have our own washing machines, own cars, own heating and cooling system, and everything is on our own. Sink or swim, it's up to us, but we are not engineered for such solitude and need the celebration of community and the warmth of the hearth. Sacred rituals provide this community togetherness and celebration, and we move close to the heart of our humanness as a result.

Invite the fire element into your life to discern its tendency in your makeup. Are you fickle and discriminating about with whom you like to hang out? Let fire illuminate your patterns of choice and examine if we are cutting off the heart of our existence.

The Directional Intentions and Dedication of the Wind Element

The final element celebrated with love through this sacred ritual of Compassionate Exchange is wind. The wind element evokes many feelings in humans from irritation to eerie and haunted feelings when the winds of change are blowing. Wind current is used ceremonially to send messages, to travel by, and communicated around the world. Prayer flags and prayer wheels are traditional ways to send the message of peace on the wind.

Think about how you know the wind element, through a gentle breeze while napping to the hurricane forces of a tornado or storm. The wind is only visible through the moving of objects, the leaves, hair, clothes, feathers, and flags. However, the air we breathe is vital and carries our voice and message through time and space. Air is the element most related to change.

In one sacred ritual in Karuna, teaching on the wind, one participant who was on oxygen to support her wind illness of COPD[56] had not made the connection with air and her condition until she was standing at the mandala. She wept in joy and gratitude at the recognition of her vital dependency on air and the miracles of medical science. She had been embarrassed about needing the oxygen and resisting its usage, but somehow during the sacred ritual at the mandala, she woke up to the vitality of air.

The wind is directional and intentional and explores everything in its path. That makes it a good messenger and place to dedicate any merit gained in sacred ritual—spread it to the far sides of the world and offer it outward to others, as opposed to hoarding the merit all to ourselves.

The air element replicates our life force and is the life force of the planet, the breath of the world. Celebrate wind today and send your messages of peace and love on the winds to time in a dedication of any merit we've gathered here today.

Love and All the Elements

By bringing the outer aspect of the Five Buddha Family Mandala, the elements, into our hearts and mind, we are celebrating and exchang-

---

56 Chronic obstructive pulmonary disease—a chronic inflammatory lung disease.

ing with the most vital forces of our existence. Simple sacred ritual is medicine for the heart, inviting us into a tremendous elemental collaboration, one in which we are already participating daily.

While living in Slovenia for almost four years in the late '90s, a time when that country was still individuating from former Yugoslavia, I found myself a stranger in a strange land. I had come to Slovenia for love and was living with my boyfriend's family in a small village called Podcerkev. I was not having an easy time—first as an American, and because everything I was doing at the time (Karuna Training) was happening a 16-hour train ride away in Germany. I decided to do a ritual atop a sacred hill called Divine just outside of Podcerkev.

I took some juniper and a mala[57] and was going to contemplate what the hell I was doing in Slovenia. I started a charcoal to burn the juniper and was doing a chant with my eyes closed when suddenly, I looked up and the charcoal had sparked a small fire that was burning down the hill in a couple of directions it appeared. I panicked and unmindfully spilled the entire burning pot of juniper over; then I had a real fire on my hands. I tried to stomp it out, but that wasn't enough, so I ended up rolling all over it to put it out. This made me covered head to toe in suet and ash. I looked like I had been through a battle when I came down the hill. But I got the message, which was to get into the soil of the place, take it on fully and completely, which I ended up doing. I studied the language and the history and planted a garden and walked the endless miles of trails there. I did long retreats, as there was actually very little to do in Slovenia except for work with your mind. Especially as an impatient, privileged,

---

57 Tibetan meditation beads have 108 beads per strand.

and entitled American, Slovenia had a few things to teach me about patience and living close to the elements.

Learning to appreciate and exchange with the potency of the elemental forces, as correlated with the Five Buddha Families, is an exercise in balancing our inner energies with the outer energetic dimensions of the world. Of course, forever, when we embark on spiritual work, we want to jump straight to the mind and heart, but there is always an interim step. That step has to do with appreciating the makeup of who and what we are, as we are—and that is elemental magic.

May your love of the elements awaken and may you commune directly with space and all its inhabitants. May the elements wake you and shake you and share with you the fruits of a life worth living.

CHAPTER XVI

Living with Eco-Anxiety*

Beginning in the late 20th century, and especially in the early 21st century, a growing body of eco-psychological knowledge has emerged in response to humanity's growing awareness of the climate crisis. Psychologists, in seeking to normalize and to label what they view as a growing emotional dysregulation due to climate change, have proposed labels such as "eco-distress," "eco-melancholia," and "eco-anxiety."[58] Recently, the American Psychiatric Association (APA) adopted "eco-anxiety" as a "chronic fear of environmental doom."[59]

Another definition of eco-anxiety is a "persistent worry about the future of the earth and the life it shelters."[60] Eco-psychology is concerned with

---

*The content in this chapter was originally published in *The Arrow: A Journal of Wakeful Society, Culture & Politics* in August, 2021.

58 Figueres, Christina and Rivett-Carnac, Tom, *The Future We Choose: Surviving the Climate Crisis* (London: Manilla Press, 2020) and Lertzman, Renee, *Environmental Melancholia: Psychoanalytic Dimensions of Engagement* (New York: Routledge, 2015).

59 Huizen, Jennifer, "What to Know About Eco-Anxiety," *Medical News Today*, December 19, 2019, https://www.medicalnewstoday.com/articles/327354.

60 Raypol, Crystal, "Climate Change Taking a Toll on Your Mental Health? How to Cope with 'Eco-Anxiety,'" *Healthline*, September 22, 2020, https://www.healthline.com/health/eco-anxiety.

human psychological relationships with nature and how eco-events, like natural disasters, impact individual and community well-being and overall health, especially in terms of personality and identity.

Environmentalist Renee Lertzman conceptualizes eco-anxiety, or what she terms environmental melancholia, to be at the heart of our apparent apathy and helplessness as a species in the face of impending doom. "Environmental melancholia—an arrested, inchoate form of mourning—is at the heart of much of the inaction in response to ecological degradation," argues Lertzman.[61] She advocates for *emotional integration*—the ability to bring awareness to emotional intensity—in order to deal with our collective trauma. According to Lertzman, emotional integration is the only way humans will be able to adapt in the face of impending disaster.

From a Contemplative Psychology perspective, working with eco-anxiety is similar to working with heightened emotions. The contemplative method leans into feelings energetically as they arise, staying with the emotional sensation instead of thinking about the issues or ruminating in fear. This methodology powerfully demonstrates that eco-anxiety is an expression of sanity; the antidote is to feel genuine grief over the state of the world as it is arising.

Contemplative Psychology offers a compassionate and mindful approach to working with anxiety, as opposed to pathologizing an individual's experience and response to the reality at hand.[62] This approach to psychology regards anxiety not as a medical diagnosis,

---

61 Lertzman, Renee, *Environmental Melancholia: Psychoanalytic Dimensions of Engagement* (New York: Routledge, 2015).

62 Trungpa Chögyam, *The Sanity We Are Born With: A Buddhist Approach to Psychology* (Boston & London: Shambhala, 2005).

but rather as a rational response to climate change. Severe instances, however, can have a mental health impact if left without alleviation.[63] A severe case can debilitate one into states of catatonia or agoraphobia due to extreme anxiety.

The climate crisis feels personal even when one has not been personally affected by fires, devastating weather events, or hurricanes. It is increasingly difficult to ignore the apocalyptic imagery of devastation that the weather is unceasingly delivering in our daily headlines. In mid-August 2020, in the heart of Denver, Colorado, Sloan's Lake, the place where I go every day to resource myself, had a significant drop in oxygen levels in the water due to the high stagnant heat and fire smoke throughout Colorado. The result was that hundreds, if not thousands, of fish died and floated to the surface. On my morning walk, I met the stench of dead fish two blocks away. The fish were lying on their bellies gasping for oxygen—mimicking the gasping for oxygen that COVID-19-inflicted patients experience. There is no air; we can't breathe.

Ecological mishaps tend to motivate action when they affect us directly in our backyard.[64] A large majority of Americans have lived through a major fire, an earthquake, a flood, or a hurricane.[65] That or we came close enough to know that the disruption is a daunting

---

63 Hoggett Paul, ed., *Climate Psychology: On Indifference to Disaster* (New York: Palgrave Macmillan, 2019).

64 Raypol, Crystal "Climate Change Taking a Toll on Your Mental Health?" *Healthline*, September 22, 2020.

65 Grieser, Justin, "Report: 243 Million Americans Affected by Weather Disasters Since 2007," *The Washington Post*, April 9, 2013, https://www.washingtonpost.com/news/capital-weather-gang/wp/2013/04/09/report-243-million-americans-affected-by-weather-disasters-since-2007/.

one. Eco-anxiety is now in the weave of the human fabric, something we are living with daily.[66]

These haunting incidents occur with such frequency that we can learn to dread the news.[67] If one believes in science, it becomes apparent that it is only getting worse. The crisis is upon us! We live with these climate change events as if one has been diagnosed with a terrible disease with a poor prognosis; we are frozen by not knowing what we can do to help. We know that unless we did something yesterday, it will continue to worsen.

In spite of the pressing need to champion ecological issues, I confess my own inconsistent activism, and the extent to which a constantly changing focus around personal habits is mired in the tiresome discourse of political correctness. I tend to move in wide swings of extremism: one year eradicating all paper in my house (except toilet paper), another time living in a permaculture food forest in California while paying high water bills. I fly to offer seminars worldwide and agonize over my carbon footprint while doing so, but I don't stop.

Many people become intentionally inactive and ignore the situation altogether, falling into what Dr. Lertzman calls the "hope and despair option." Rather than motivating action, this option leaves us wallowing in ambivalence and paralysis. For many, the eco-crisis presents a significant concern—a large majority of Americans are

---

66 Lertzman, Renee, *Environmental Melancholia: Psychoanalytic Dimensions of Engagement* (New York: Routledge, 2015).

67 Figueres, Christina and Rivett-Carnac, Tom, *The Future We Choose: Surviving the Climate Crisis* (London: Manilla Press, 2020) and Lertzman, Renee, Environmental Melancholia: Psychoanalytic Dimensions of Engagement (New York: Routledge, 2015).

concerned about climate change and growing numbers see it as a crisis.[68] More and more people have responded by becoming vegan, creating gardens, choosing local community-supported agriculture, and even deciding not to bear offspring. Still, those of us with comforts and conveniences constantly find ourselves head-to-head with the paradox of feeling that we should give them up.[69]

It is challenging to bear the truth of the crisis consciously and consistently. It is easy to grow ambivalent and complacent just to keep ourselves and our families healthy and housed.[70] During the COVID-19 pandemic, I've found many of my behaviors increasingly at odds with my environmental and ethical commitments. For example, I order way too much from Amazon when it appears to be the only place to get what I want. Convenience facilitates becoming unconscious of the urgency of the challenges we face.

Contemplative Psychology calls for facing and feeling the underbelly of our anxiety and resourcing ourselves in doing so. Resourcing means we take a pause to integrate our emotional reactions through experiencing them fully and completely. Usually, when we are hit with an emotional reaction, we either bury them or act them out; however, resourcing means we integrate the feelings fully by giving the energy our attention. We offer ourselves a kind and open space

---

68 Brady, Dennis, Mufson, Steven, and Clement, Scott, "Americans Increasingly See Climate Change as a Crisis, Poll Shows," *The Washington Post*, September 13, 2019, https://www.washingtonpost.com/climate-environment/americans-increasingly-see-climate-change-as-a-crisis-poll-shows/2019/09/12/74234db0-cd2a-11e9-87fa-8501a456c003_story.html.

69 Figueres, Christina and Rivett-Carnac, Tom, *The Future We Choose: Surviving the Climate Crisis* (London: Manilla Press, 2020).

70 Lertzman, Renee, *Environmental Melancholia: Psychoanalytic Dimensions of Engagement* (New York: Routledge, 2015).

to experience emotional energy as it is, completely. This is the Contemplative Psychology approach to working with emotions—we integrate them and utilize the energy as a strength.

We cannot advance any of our aspirations to make a change or to consciously steward the environment without learning to relate directly with eco-anxieties. If we do not embrace the emotions we are sitting with, we will never be consistent or successful in changing habits that need changing.[71]

For those of us who experience eco-anxiety, step one is to meet and feel that anxiety directly for what it is: helplessness, fear, stubbornness, or attachment. We need to take the time to touch all aspects of what exists and why we feel the anxiety we do. Karen Kissel Wegela reminds us that "the very things we do to become confused can be turned around and used to help us reconnect to our brilliant sanity."[72] The problem is that meeting our anxiety is the last thing most of us want to do. Often, we look for anything, any fix we can find not to feel the tinge of anxiety.

Emotions arise as messages, and they are full of wisdom when we're not using emotions to confirm that we exist. If we avoid or micro-manage emotions, then they govern us like demons; ultimately, however, emotions are our teachers. The way to meet our emotional energy directly is to feel our emotions as they arise by listening to the body, as opposed to the thoughts in our head.

---

71 Wegela, Karen Kissel, *How to Be a Help Instead of a Nuisance: Practical Approaches to Giving Support, Service, and Encouragement to Others* (Boston & London: Shambhala, 1996).

72 Wegela, Karen Kissel, *How to Be a Help Instead of a Nuisance: Practical Approaches to Giving Support, Service, and Encouragement to Others* (Boston & London: Shambhala, 1996).

Learning how to do this is a contemplative discipline; it takes mind training—building the muscle of awareness that habituates us to come back to our bodies as an anchor. Learning to feel the energy of emotions.[73]

In using Contemplative Psychology methods, such as meeting our emotions directly, it is essential to be gentle and kind toward ourselves. The practice is to befriend our emotional energy and learn to listen to emotional pain simply as information rather than as an obstruction.[74]

We need a robust, supportive environment and a means by which we can resource ourselves to be brave and experience the wisdom of underlying painful emotions.[75] A supportive environment can take many forms, but at minimum, it must be a place where we feel protected enough to address genuine emotional depth. Sometimes a class or a group dedicated to grieving our planet's loss can be helpful.[76] For myself, I've created Contemplative Psychology-inspired groups to support us in exploring how to live with our emotional energy related to the environment on a day-to-day basis. The entire curriculum of Karuna Training occurs in a cohort over the course of two years, allowing participants to bring many issues, environmental

73 Trungpa, Chögyam, *The Sanity We Are Born With: A Buddhist Approach to Psychology* (Boston: Shambhala, 2005); Chödrön, Pema, *The Wisdom of No Escape and the Path of Loving-Kindness* (Boston & London: Shambhala, 1991).

74 Trungpa, Chögyam, *The Sanity We Are Born With: A Buddhist Approach to Psychology* (Boston & London: Shambhala, 2005); Chödrön, Pema, *The Wisdom of No Escape and the Path of Loving-Kindness* (Boston: Shambhala, 1991).

75 Trungpa, Chögyam, *The Sanity We Are Born With: A Buddhist Approach to Psychology* (Boston & London: Shambhala, 2005).

76 Lertzman, Renee, *Environmental Melancholia: Psychoanalytic Dimensions of Engagement* (New York: Routledge, 2015).

anxiety as only one issue, as a topic to be held and related to in the community. When we work in a community, the opportunity is one of "being heard" and "bearing witness" to others' emotional truths. This communal listening strengthens us and supports the further capacity to meet and hear others in their pain.

When we face our fears, anxiety, and complacency and dare to feel them directly, we strengthen fearlessness because we are daring to feel emotions directly and fully on the spot. Facing fear can look like a breakdown or display of vulnerability on the surface, but the willingness to feel unpleasant emotional energy builds strength and resilience. Meeting this energy directly empowers us; we derive resourcefulness within ourselves by facing and feeling our emotions.[77]

It is essential to find a community with whom we can rally to restore our faith and resource ourselves for the immense challenges humanity currently faces. Multiple ecological grief groups are forming—online salons and Google groups designed to help us collectively process the ways in which we live in and out of alignment with our values. We need support: domains to hold the truth of our changing relationship to climate and the ecological challenges ahead of us because it is nearly impossible to bear it alone.[78]

For example, the day I discovered the dead fish in Sloan's Lake, I was fortunate to attend an ecology group with whom I could share my feelings about what happened. The ability to talk about it strengthened me such that from the moment I left the group, I could move

---

77 Wegela, Karen Kissel, *How to Be a Help Instead of a Nuisance: Practical Approaches to Giving Support, Service, and Encouragement to Others* (Boston & London: Shambhala, 1996).

78 Lertzman, Renee, *Environmental Melancholia: Psychoanalytic Dimensions of Engagement* (New York: Routledge, 2015).

beyond my shock and begin to investigate what happened and what could be done. My initial research, however, led me to a good deal of speculation from my neighbors on Nextdoor posts, from "someone put some blue chemicals in the water" to "the lake is dead and the spring has dried up." These speculations were pure anxiety speaking—yet another opportunity to look beneath impulsive, reactive fears and discover what is happening in our own minds and in the broader situation. Once we can discern our true feelings and bolster/brace/ground/reinforce ourselves enough to investigate a situation thoroughly, then and only then can we ask the question, "What can I do?"

To work with my anxiety around the lake, I again turned to Nextdoor, but this time I started my own channel, "Let's Help Sloan's Lake," on the Nextdoor app. In starting this channel, I've collected people with much more information and learned that the problem is greater than I imagined: Not only has the lake lost its original spring, but the neighborhood runoff is what provides the water in the lake. Often when we examine a situation more deeply, we end up peeling back a layer of hidden truths and find out even worse news.

Ultimately, it is essential that the work of addressing eco-anxiety extends to feelings one's feelings directly and authentically, as well as doing so in a like-minded community. Thus, preparing ourselves for a journey where we can make whatever changes we think are appropriate and in accord with our values. On my daily walks to the lake, I now keenly keep an eye on water levels and the lake's general health. I see the face of Sloan's Lake change daily, and recently the lake appears healthier due to extreme late winter snowfall. However, I know the lake's apparent health is an illusion.

Living with eco-anxiety is about tuning in to the environment and holding nature along with ourselves in loving-kindness. It is a journey of realizing the anxiety is accurate and there's a reason it's coming up—it is intelligence! The environment is speaking to us, the elements are raging from a human perspective, and the real question is, are we listening?

To live with eco-anxiety is to embrace the notion that we are interconnected with this sacred earth and all its inhabitants. Their health and sanity are directly related to our health and sanity. When we begin to feel into and embrace our planet and its inhabitants as a family, we naturally want to find ways to act; even small changes work to make a difference and help to ease our anxiety. The connection we have with the environment abides in the heart, flourishes in the mind, and lives through the body.

We all need to find ways to stay focused and staying focused is 99 percent of the effort.

CHAPTER XVII

Embracing Transitions

I took care of my mother when she was declining due to Alzheimer's over the last four and a half years of her life. I saw to her comfort as best I could, without moving her into my house and ruining my marriage. My marriage ended anyway. The death of my mother exposed the deficits in my marriage, and my life, as death is prone to do. When my mother passed, a whole phase of life passed with her.

I sat by my mother's bed saying mantras,[79] as we both experienced her labored breathing. The breathing was one of someone dosed heavily with morphine. Any little stirring, in fact, invited the nurses to dose her with more morphine. I told myself they were ushering her out gently, but it remains a question in my mind about anesthetizing one's passing as the status quo! What are we deeply avoiding? I know my mother was in pain, so I was grateful for the morphine too, but it is not so simple.

---

79 Mantra—a Tibetan word meaning "mind protection." Typically, a mantra goes with a deity and each mantra has a purpose, for peace, love, intellect, wish-fulfilling, etc.

In one moment, she was deliriously fighting invisible demons, and then she would let go in exhaustion. Another moment fidgeting and struggling in her discomfort to breathe. I continued saying mantras by her bed and exchanging with her with as much love and basic sanity as I could rouse. Occasionally I would say, "It's okay to let go, Mom. I'm here. I love you. You've lived a good, long life; we are at peace now."

Another moment, her last moment of being fully cognizant, she uncharacteristically reached toward me to push a strand of hair behind my ear. It was a motherly gesture I had not known from her in life. Usually, we did not exhibit such loving expressions. Nevertheless, it was a loving gesture and she asked me, "Are you praying?" "Yes, Mom, I'm praying for your safe passage so you can be peaceful and open in your transition." Then, very characteristically, she harumphed and said, "You need a haircut!" Those were my mother's last words to me. She died the next day while I sat beside her continuing to say mantras.

My best friend, Charles, appeared right on cue, literally the moment she passed. He was there with me to sit with her body in the immediate transition. Charles had known my mom since we were in our early 20s, longer than any of my friends. Charles knew the whole dynamic of our relationship, and he had a soft spot for my mother. After some time, we went to have breakfast and ate a huge stack of pancakes because we were ravenous. It was so good that my friend was there with me to be sad together during her impactful transition.

As Francis Weller says, "Sorrow helps us remember something long intuited by indigenous people across the planet: Our lives are intricately connected with one another, with animals, plants, watersheds, and soil."[80] The need to touch into the ordinariness of death, some-

---

80 Weller, Francis, *The Wild Edge of Sorrow: Rituals of Renewal and the Sacred Work of Grief* (Berkeley: North Atlantic Books, 2015), p. xvi.

thing that is interconnected with all species, ferries us through life's most potent moments. Death is very natural, and its greatest value is in being witnessed and shared. Transitions connect us to the heart of community, to family, and to a deep realization that we all matter, and our passing does impact the greater whole.

This chapter discusses the role of Compassionate Exchange in transitions, and how exchanging self with others in the pauses, gaps, goodbyes, terminations, deaths, and dissolving relationships leads us to a fulfilled communal heart. A heart with which we are all longing to connect.

Naming the Bardo

I've said many times while teaching in Karuna Training on transition: *all relationships are made dynamic by the truth of their impending death.* What is significant is whether we appreciate people in life and whether we take continuity for granted. When a relationship has ceased to be precious, we aren't appreciating its impermanence. Recalling all the times I've slipped away from my loved ones, without any acknowledgment of their importance to me, I was ignoring the potency and transmutational properties of the in-between states.

In Tibetan Buddhism, these transitions are referred to as a bardo state, and there are many bardos identified: the Bardo of Life, the Bardo of the Dream State, the Bardo of Meditation, the Bardo of Death, the Bardo of the State After Death, and the Bardo of Becoming or Rebirth. There is a wealth of writings available on these bardos, by people with far more understanding and insight than me. I have benefited from the discussion of bardos by Chögyam Trungpa, who encouraged a practical approach: bardo or transition as opportunity, no matter the title or when it is occurring.

The Tibetan word refers to in-between states. Trungpa elaborates: "Bar means 'in-between' or you could say, 'no-man's-land,' and 'do' is like a tower or an island in the no-man's-land. It's like a flowing river that belongs to neither the other shore nor to this shore, but there is an island in the middle, in between. In other words, it is a present moment experience, the immediate experience of nowness—where you are, where you're at. That is the basic idea of bardo."[81]

Bardos are named so we can acknowledge with awareness the change of consciousness occurring during a particular period in our existence. Not only can bardos be experienced solely in the present moment, but they are also constant too. If we think about it, we are forever in one transition or another. Therefore, they are a means of riding the change consciously, which helps us make more informed and awake choices moment to moment. The period when I was doing post-doctoral work was among the most difficult years I can remember. Another excruciating transition was coming back to America after living abroad for nearly a decade; it was like I had split my consciousness and the events and people on either side had no relationship to one another. I was vulnerable and thus open, not holding the experiences too tightly or self-consciously. It is during transitions like these that we have access to creative inspiration.

Paying attention to transitions is the secret sauce or active ingredient of offering ourselves in Compassionate Exchange. Over the course of training, people learn how to offer themselves selflessly to another as a Compassionate Friend. This form might look like therapy, but it's not therapy, because there is no objective to fix anything. However, the results of being deeply listened to in Compassionate Exchange

---

81 Trungpa, Chögyam, "Bardo" in "Transcending Madness" from *The Collected Works of Chögyam Trungpa, Volume 6* (Boston & London: Shambhala, 2004), p. 11.

can be healing. The practice of a Compassionate Friend is one of entering the dyad without an agenda, and this notion of "nothing to fix" can occur because we are approaching another with the view of intrinsic health. Compassionate exchange is a heart-opening practice.

In Karuna Training, we invite awareness of bardo by welcoming abrupt transitions. What I mean is that Karuna students progressing through the two-year curriculum are trained to let go and bring themselves present by the sound of the meditation gong. Participants are invited to make this abrupt transition a practice of hearing the gong and immediately they stop talking, no matter what they're saying, or how important it feels to finish the sentence, they stop and let go and come present. I always say this is a sign of a well-trained mind, when one can truly let go mid-sentence. Not because we shouldn't finish our sentences, but because by letting go we are practicing a momentary bardo and feeling the texture of that transition.

The discipline is one of dropping out of the head and into one's body and feeling the present moment in silence. Of course, there is resistance to letting go of one's words at the sound of the gong, and that too is part of building awareness, and looking at what and how we hang on to our stories and the importance of what we want to say. I consider the capacity to create an abrupt cut by dropping into silence at the sound of a gong a high accomplishment.

When we begin to understand the importance of naming a bardo, we are fearlessly willing to touch the truth of impermanence. Embracing and understanding this truth is key to embracing and working with the transformative capacities of bardos. Bardos are peak moments within a transition, and to touch that peak is to be fully present for change. To do so takes intensity capacity, the ability to stay present in one's mind during intense emotions or vulnerability. Staying present in awareness is what we're strengthening in meditation practice.

There are all kinds of deaths in life, but humans tend to fixate on the death of our bodies on the physical plane. I've often found myself thinking about the reason I took refuge as a Buddhist. I remember hearing that Buddhists meditate to prepare for their deaths.

The notion of rebirth was introduced in a course on the Tibetan bardos at Naropa Institute. I found out that Buddhists believe sentient beings choose their rebirth. That these choices are closely linked to our current consciousness and how consciously we live our lives. A free and well-favored rebirth depends on one's ability to choose wisely; to be of benefit to others in life is the goal, once we progress on the Buddhist path. Meditation is the choice practice to train in being present during our death so that we can choose properly with awareness in the bardo.

I'm not realized enough to know whether choosing one's rebirth is true or not; however, I like the implications of the notion. Such an idea liberates me from the notion of destiny and puts the responsibility right on me for what I accept and reject in life, moment to moment. I've noticed I end up choosing the same partner over and over, only with a different name. Over time, the same difficulties and relational issues reoccur and are often more exaggerated than in my last relationship. I understand the Buddhist teachings on rebirth on a moment-to-moment basis, versus lifetime to lifetime. We choose our rebirth every moment when we understand this view.

There are numerous other types of death beyond our physical one. There are emotional deaths, like when we cease to feel anything for another person. Or perhaps we have experienced being "ghosted" by someone who has decided we're no longer worthy of being friends. Ghosted is a slang term that vividly captures the experience of getting no response once we've reached out to another. When ghosted, we often feel abandoned and discarded. One can only imagine the emotional impact of social media on children and young adults these days, who undoubtedly are being ghosted and befriended at the rate of a heartbeat. Imagine the impact!

It is excruciatingly painful to find out that a long-term relationship no longer means what it originally did to either you or another person. We're often shocked to find out there is a lack of investment on the part of family, friends, or ex-lovers and we've intentionally been ignored by them. We seem, culturally, to give family members a free pass to ghost one another, like a new normal. This distancing is often an intelligent means of self-preservation; however, it is sad because until only recently, we needed our neighbors, friends, and families for the hardships of life, deaths, births, and emergencies. Only in the last 70 years, since mid-century post-World War II, have we been able to fully ignore our neighbors, given the growth of consumerism and how we have each set up our own little kingdom to fend for ourselves.

Sometimes we completely forget about others—out of sight, out of mind. These are a type of mental death. These are transitions where we totally cease to be aware any longer of someone or something. This could be a dissociative adaptation due to trauma, or it could be the medicine of space and time that heals a trauma when something has been truly integrated, and we no longer need to ruminate on the pain.

The Power of Discerning Transition

Discerning transitions during exchange is about riding the present through feeling within and oscillating in and out of the experience of another. The technique of oscillation works to heighten the detection of transitions happening in the present moment. Discerning transitions means pausing and feeling into the empty spaces, the gaps, and feeling the pregnancy of the moment. In Compassionate Exchange we become shepherds of transitions, and we do so by riding open space with awareness.

Discerning transition requires staying with energy, specifically the energy of open space, which most of the time, we discern as a death. As we learn to pause and experience these gaps, even when it feels uncomfortable, we are building intensity capacity for discomfort.

For years, I ran group processes, first with clients in clinics, and then later with students in Karuna. Over time, I've learned about the potency of discerning and staying with transitions. These potent moments are full of potential and deep connection, although they are also full of vulnerability. Group participants often feel fear because of the silence in a conversation, which is what they are often avoiding. That is how superficial chatter works: it fills the space and helps people avoid discomfort.

However, when a container has been set in a contemplative group setting and the rules are established, we're speaking from the heart and only saying that which we want to be heard and witnessed by others. There is no cross-talk and no questions, just deep feeling and listening to others' experience in the group. Then the situations heighten and the silences grow. There is usually a certain amount of vulnerability in these silences, and that is where the power abides, but sometimes people are too wounded to display their vulnerability.

In Contemplative Psychology, we understand that, paradoxically, our strength is found amid our vulnerability. And the daringness to touch our open, often-wounded heart is the source from which we find our greatest resilience and basic sanity.

The capacity to stay present with potent pregnant transitions is a skill in Contemplative Psychology, especially awkward transitions, when people run out of things to say or they feel emotional, embarrassed, and suddenly self-conscious. Staying with these bardos openly, without agenda, and nonjudgmentally allows for the completeness of another's expression. Space allows the safety of one's vulnerability to be touched.

By paying attention to the bardos of beginnings and endings in Compassionate Exchange, and by making space for all the mini-deaths in the middle, we're attuning to the natural flow of birth and death. Attuning to transition during a conversation isn't done self-consciously but as part of a natural oscillation of paying attention to our exchange with others. When we can do so, the practice of oscillation reveals how comfortable we are in the flow of change. We learn a lot about another's relationship to space by attuning to the many bardos that arise during a Compassionate Exchange.

We instigate transitions when we end a Compassionate Exchange session. In Compassionate Exchange, we strive for a non-agenda-driven container offered by the compassionate friend, and yet bringing a conversation to a proper end is also creating a work of art. What is most important when ending a Compassionate Exchange is acknowledging the death, reiterating the purpose of the work you've done together, and remembering the shared agreement (if there is one). It is powerful, as a Compassionate Friend, to offer the person who was sharing experience a brief oral summary of all the highlights the two of you discussed, especially what has stuck with you during the Compassionate Exchange. The transition is then highlighted with a brief summary of what has transpired and allows the person who shared to reflect more deeply on what they've said and what has been heard. This display of generosity is one of deep listening and offering of a reflection—we are bearing witness to another's heart.

Practicing Compassionate Exchange is being a shepherd of transitions, and becoming a shepherd of transitions requires a lot of awareness and applied practice, or we miss the subtlety. Many people in Compassionate Exchange have affirmed how they've never felt listened to before doing this practice. People also tell me they've never ended anything properly in their lives before this practice and begin to realize that they've warded off a natural sadness around death and the joy of appreciating the passing of something or someone properly. They realize they have forgone the blessing of space.

Chögyam Trungpa called this blessing of combining sadness and joy developing a *genuine heart of sadness*. "Ordinarily, when you talk about feeling sad, it means you are so hurt; you feel so bad. When you talk about feeling joyous, it means that you feel so excited and uplifted. Here you develop sadness and joy at once."[82] The genuine heart of sadness is often experienced as sad-joy, sadness because we are willing to touch our vulnerability in transitions, and joy because we are developing confidence in doing so. It is also excellent when one's genuine heart of sadness can be exchanged in the practice of Compassionate Exchange. One feels witnessed, connected, and part of humanity when that occurs.

---

82 Trungpa, Chögyam, "How to Cultivate the Great Eastern Sun" from *Great Eastern Sun: The Wisdom of Shambhala* (Boston & London: Shambhala, 2001), pp. 110–111.

The Practice of Embracing Transitions

Below I offer ordinary practices for cultivating awareness and appreciation of transitions.

We can start by learning to say goodbye. It can be difficult to say goodbye genuinely because to do so is acknowledging a death. Some of us are efficient in ignoring any goodbyes.

For the many years during which I worked in treatment facilities, I ran groups, primarily women's groups, targeted at wellness or toward the pathology of whatever the women were there for and for which they were receiving treatment. Inevitably, almost weekly, someone was discharging and asked me to opt out of the last group. I always told them the last group was the most important one because it's when we get to say goodbye properly.

I asked each participant to say goodbye to each person, both individually and as a group. This took some time and often elicited a lot of emotions, often surprising to the client. The practice was in addressing one another directly and bothering to say what was true and genuine in that moment of the relationship. Often these women had been in treatment for months and so they were leaving a community, for better or worse. For many clients, this exercise was excruciating for demanding something from them they had spent a lifetime avoiding.

Training ourselves to acknowledge and speak to transitions when they're occurring is simply good psychological hygiene. It's bothering to say goodbye properly to those with whom we love, even though we expect to see them later in the day. What if we don't make it home? Or they don't make it home? Contemplating the truth of impermanence is a strong motivation for saying goodbye.

Another practice is to contemplate the transition you are currently in in our life due to time and age. For example, consider what has ended, when there is nothing yet begun. Post-graduation, post-marriage, post serving time in the military or foreign service, post coming home from living abroad, post children leaving for college, or moving out for good. There are so many life transitions to acknowledge and consider when taking account of our overall life transitions.

One can simply contemplate the transitions in one's day, which if we are commuting or traveling can be illusory.

Many nights in my mid-50s, while working and commuting to San Francisco, I anticipated not being able to sleep, a serious problem. Having traveled through so many different scenes and scenarios in one day, I was able to hypnotize myself to sleep by reviewing the bardos of my day: I recalled rising at home with my animals and cozy existence in small-town Petaluma. Dreading the congested commute, especially if I am only getting on the road by 7 a.m. Not to mention the dread of the meetings to follow and things to do once at work. Getting on the road and making a significant phone call or speaking with a good friend for the one- to two-hour drive to the city could be exhilarating. Arriving at work. Going immediately to my office to pull myself together for the day. Meeting with my thousand-armed deity administrative assistant and having her dictate a good portion of my day and phone calls to make. Sometimes driving to the East Bay or south to Silicon Valley, or into the front lines of homeless services in San Francisco.

Often the end of the day became blurred in my mind, sometimes forgetting my house in Petaluma, forgetting my garden, my kind husband, my two dogs, two cats, chickens, bees, and the basic sanity of home. The odd paradox that haunted me in the transitions was the amount of work I was doing to keep everything I was missing afloat! When I took time to contemplate these discordant daily transitions while falling asleep, I drifted off somewhere in the day out of pure exhaustion.

One final and highly recommended practice is also to track the space between your thoughts during meditation, and there are many methods to do so. Malas[83] are good for following one breath and seeing how many beads one stays present. Constancy and practice are the best medicine.

Sitting in meditation, the vital central chord of the mala of this book, is core to waking up to the potency of transition as well as the nature of time. Time harnesses our minds into believing it is solid when it's merely a conceptual construct that we collectively agree to follow. Time is practical and has deep mystical aspects because it seems to expand and contract depending on our state of mind.

I recommend taking between two and four weeks to practice a long meditation retreat. This is one way we get to know oneself well and practice a discipline that's not about improving or fixing ourselves but, rather, coming to terms with ourselves as we are. It can be boring and maddening, crazy-making, depending on who is holding the container and how strict they apply the rules. A month of sitting meditation is also a descent into discipline and is highly recommended for the practitioner of Contemplative Psychology. The purpose of meditating is to make friends with oneself and to settle into the subtlety of death in every moment. Meditation offers us a rich experience of watching our mind move and transition in and out of brilliant sanity.

---

83 Mala—a Tibetan meditation tool that consists of 108 threaded beads.

In closing, I offer this book to those seeking a way to evoke basic sanity in their daily lives, especially in their relationships with others. The methods I've pointed to here, when practiced with regularity, create a kind and intelligent connection with oneself and an opulent open-hearted relationship with others. The book is specially written for those of you who struggle with difficult emotions. I've learned from the many students of Karuna Training that Contemplative Psychology is a path unto itself, and that one doesn't have to be a Buddhist or a care provider for the methods to be life-transforming.

I often tell people, "What I teach in Karuna Training should be taught in kindergarten." I believe Contemplative Psychology offers profound methods of kindness, open-heartedness, and compassionate collaboration that we are sorely lacking in humanity's common knowledge. Contemplative Psychology not only teaches us how to communicate more effectively but also serves as a means to resource ourselves with our emotions, as opposed to being driven by them.

The world is undergoing rapid and intense challenges at present—perhaps this is always true—but, currently, in modern society, we are more interconnected than ever due to the miracles of the internet. This makes the world a much smaller place, and there is more need to work together to meet the modern challenges of our time. How we live together, share resources, and make emotional room for the daunting changes upon us as a global community matters! Finding a way to live in harmony and with genuine heart may be the only hope for our species.

I want to say goodbye to my readers as I often end my Karuna Trainings . . .

Go gently and lead with your heart!

About the Author

Melissa Moore, PhD, is an educator and has dedicated her life to teaching Buddhism and Contemplative Psychology. She has a master's degree from Naropa University in Contemplative Psychotherapy and a PhD from California Institute of Integral Studies in San Francisco in Psychological Anthropology. She has been a student of Chögyam Trungpa Rinpoche since the age of 25 and has been a senior teacher in the Shambahla community for the past 30 years.

Melissa is co-founder of Karuna Training, a certification in Contemplative Psychology, which has been offered as a cohort training since 1996 in eight countries: DE, NL, FR, AU, PO, SP, UK, and USA. Melissa has been teaching Contemplative Psychology in Karuna for the past 27 years all over the United States, Europe, Australia, and New Zealand. She is currently the executive director of Karuna North America, http://www.karunatraining.com.

In addition to her Buddhist teaching, Melissa has held many positions in mental health, most recently as the founding director of the Felton Institute in San Francisco, California. She completed a post-doctoral degree in 2005 at the University of California San Francisco in a program dedicated to community-based research in mental health, and from that program arose the Felton Institute. The objective of the Felton Institute was to train the least experienced frontline providers in community mental health services in evidence-based practices and then to research the results of that training. Melissa spent many years working as a treatment specialist in eating disorders and issues of women's abuse. Melissa currently lives in Denver, Colorado, with her husband and dog.

Suggested Further Reading on Contemplative Psychology

Chögyam Trungpa

Trungpa, Chögyam, *The Collected Works of Chögyam Trungpa*, Volumes 1, 2, 3, 4, 5, 6, 7, 8, Shambhala Publications, 2003–2004.

Trungpa, Chögyam, *The Sanity We Are Born With*, Shambhala Publications, Boston, London, 2005.

Trungpa, Chögyam, *Training the Mind and Cultivating Loving-Kindness; The Main Practice Which Is Training Bodhichitta*, Shambhala Publications, 1993.

Trungpa, Chögyam, *The Bodhisattva Path of Wisdom and Compassion: The Profound Treasury of the Ocean of Dharma*, Volume One & Two.

Dr. Ed Podvoll, MD

Podvoll, Edward, MD, *Recovering Sanity: A Compassionate Approach to Understanding and Treating Psychosis*, previously published as *The Seduction of Madness*, HarperCollins, New York, 1990.

Podvoll, Edward, MD, *The Seduction of Madness: Revolutionary Insights into the World of Psychosis and a Compassionate Approach to Recovery at Home*, HarperCollins, New York, 1990.

Other authors on Contemplative Psychology

Chapman, Susan Gillis, *The Five Keys to Mindful Communication*, Shambhala Publications, Boston, 2021.

Chödrön, Pema, *Start Where You Are: A Guide to Compassionate Living*, Shambhala Publications, 1994.

Chödrön, Pema, *When Things Fall Apart*, Shambhala Publications, 2003.

Chögyam, Ngakpa, with Khandro Dechen, *Spectrum of Ecstasy*, Shambhala Publications, Boston, London, 2003.

Fremantle, Francesca, *Luminous Emptiness*, Shambhala Publications, 2001.

Kolts, Russel and Chodron, Thubten, *An Open-Hearted Life*. Shambhala Publications, Boston, 2015.

Kornfield, Jack, *The Wise Heart: A Guide to the Universal Teachings of Buddhist Psychology*, Bantam Books, 2008.

O'Neil, James, *Undressing*, Short Books, London, 2019.

Wegela, Karen Kissel, *How to Be a Help instead of a Nuisance: Practical Approaches to Giving Support, Service, and Encouragement to Others*, Shambhala Publications, Boston, 1996.

Acknowledgments

This book was sparked through conversations with my Karuna Training colleague and editor, Emily Earlenbaugh, PhD. Emily engaged my voice as a writer by offering to edit Karuna newsletters. In this way, she gently ushered in my confidence as a writer and as someone with something to say. For that push I'm eternally grateful—thank you!

I want to also take the time to thank my Karuna colleagues who have been instrumental in shaping the journey of Contemplative Psychology as a training: first Barbara Maertens, who took over Karuna Training in 2004 and shepherded its life and growth in Europe, in multiple countries for the last 17 years. Barbara and I have spent hours chewing through the curriculum of Karuna, teaching together in seminars, and birthing experiential work in the woods of Haus Ebersburg, Germany. These are times that I will always cherish as the most gratifying collaborative work of my life. Barbara, I'm forever grateful for your friendship and the arduous push you've made to keep Karuna going over the years.

I want to thank Paul Cashman, an original teacher and long-term contributor to the curriculum of Karuna Training, and the late Gisela Von Keiser, who was instrumental in Karuna's appeal in the beginning. To Susan Chapman, who has accompanied me on this journey since our time together at Naropa and championed Karuna along with her own methodology of the Five Keys. To Sandra Ladley, who was instrumental in bringing forth Karuna North America, and Terry Jaworski, another lifelong companion on the path of

Contemplative Psychology and a classmate of mine at Naropa Institute. I want to take the opportunity to thank Chris Tamjidi who rescued Karuna at a volatile moment when I headed back to the U.S. Chris invested in the Karuna brand and nurtured it over the years, and I'm forever grateful to you for your contributions.

All these people's voices appear in this book, and I want to acknowledge them all for their input over the years and for supporting the body of work we call Karuna Training. Karuna Training would never have emerged without the strong interest and hard work of the original founding members of Upaya, Ltd: Hubert Backes, Dagmar Niehaus, Lisa Fey, Gabi Gokert, and Angelika Schulz.

For everyone listed above, I am forever grateful that our paths crossed as they did, and for your enormous dedication to the vision of brilliant sanity.

Deep Gratitude

The greatest thank you goes to all Karuna Training participants from whom I've learned the most about Contemplative Psychology over the past 27 years. A huge thank you goes to my North American Karuna colleagues. First I'm grateful to all present and past Karuna North American faculty: Anie Boudreau, Dina Buck, Susan Chapman, Emily Earlenbaugh, Marie Endres, Margot Geist, Miriam Hall, Jay Jaworski, Terry Jaworski, Sandra Ladley, Kat Larson, Barbara Lodman, Kathryn Rile, Sakti Rose, Joachim Sehrbrock, Reese Sweeny-Taylor, and Carolyn Sykes. Let me not forget the incredible administrative support of Dave Dubois, Nico Gamache Kocal, Mairead Jacobs Dougherty, Em Nelson, and Savanah Sheets, who supported me and Karuna Training in ways I could never recount here. All people mentioned above have contributed greatly to this book because I've learned so much from each one of you!

I want to thank Holly Morphew for her continual cheerleading, Catherine Gregory and Nathan Joblin of Modern Wisdom Press for their skilled guidance, and a special deep bow to my editors, Emily Earlenbaugh and my developmental editor, Gabrielle Idlet, who contributed so greatly to this work.

I want to thank close friends, former students, and Upaya board members, who read advanced copies and lent me support and direction: Mahesi Caplan, Nan Clydesdale, Gil Figueroa, Carolyn Larson Garcia, Jess Locke, and Samo Skerbec.

My deepest gratitude is to my husband and partner, Aaron Snyder, who provided me the space and ground to write this book and, most importantly, offered me loving nonjudgmental encouragement along the way—thank you!

Index

A

Absolute bodhicitta, heart space, 164
Absolute truth, 143–147
  touching, 145
Acting directly (prajna aspect), 191–193
Addiction, 24–25, 211
  pathological notion, challenge, 231
Advice-giving, platitudes (absence), 138
Afflicted consciousness (cloudy mind), 57, 58
Aggression (poison), 89, 182
  feeling/contemplation, 106
  presence, 176
  root klesha, 107
  thriving, justification (impact), 177
  transformation, 221
Aggressive energy, 106
Agoraphobia, 243
AIDS epidemic, 26–27
Aimlessly wandering, 82
Air, dependency (recognition), 236
Alaya, 58
Algorithmic clicks/interests, 47
All-accommodating action (wisdom), Karma envy (transmutation), 219–220
All-accommodating space, 90
All-encompassing space, Buddha ignorance (transmutation), 216–217

Alternative methods, questions, 230
Anger
  involvement, 111
  personalization, avoidance, 160
  suppression, habit, 112
  Vajra anger, transmutation, 220–221
Anxiety, 208
  eco-anxiety, 241
  facing, 245–246, 248
  feeling, 31, 245–246
  levels, wearing out, 117
  production, 200
  provocation, 198
Apathy, 55
Appreciation, expression, 236
Aspirations, 234–235
  advancement, impossibility, 246
Aspiring/entering, 139–143
Asylum mentality, 155
Avoidance, habits, 101
Awakened heart (Bodhicitta), 22, 98, 115–116
  growth, 124
  realization, 135–136
  types, 140
Awakeness, 142
Awareness
  building, 255
  cultivation, 24
  heart awareness, refinement, 127–129
  presence, 256
  refined awareness, cultivation, 38
  refined heart, 115
  refinement, 78, 83

F

False projections, 126
Familial conditioning, 64
Fan and the sword, 183
  exchange, 188
Fear
  examination, 249
  experience, 212
  facing, 248
  feeling, silence (presence), 258
  rumination, 242
Feelings
  avoidance/ignoring, 135
  blockage, 130
  change, 63
  learning, 69
  messiness, 135
  resonance, ability, 197
Feeling Skandha (second Skandha),
  55, 90–91, 203
Feeling-types, 86, 99
Felt-sense, 116
Fifth Skandha
  (consciousness), 56–57
  map, 58
Figueres, Christina, 241, 244, 245
Fire, 232
  celebration/magnetism, 235–236
  Five Buddha Families elemental
    energy, 226
  Tibetan element, 35, 144
First Skandha, 54, 216
Five Buddha Families, 82, 88
  associations/attributes, 94–95
  division/study, 221
  energy, 200–201
  Five Skandhas, correlation, 89
  kleshas, correlation, 107
  knowing/not knowing, 200–202
  mandala, 76

Skandhas, connection, 213
  understanding, 89–95
Five Buddha Family Maitri
  Rooms, 85
Five Buddha Family Mandala,
  90–92, 225–226
  context, 227
  styles, 87
  translation, 92
  usage, 229–230
Five poisons, 89
Five Skandhas, Five Buddha
  Families (correlation), 89
Floyd, George (murder), 178
Fluidity (unbound openness),
  understanding/experience, 46–47
Fluid, unbound openness
  (alternative), 47
Formation (Skandha), 92
For-profit medicine career,
  cessation, 14
Four Limitless Capacities of
  Heart, 116
Four Potencies of Heart, 118–125
Four-Step Practice, 97, 101–102,
  109, 186
  usage, 102, 103, 211
Fourth Skandha (intellect), 56
Fremantle, Francesca, 122, 142
Freud, Sigmund, 10–11, 67,
  154–155
Frustration, 100

G

Generosity, 234–235
  impact, 176
Generosity Paramita, 170–174
Genuine compassion, rarity, 160

I

Made in the USA
Middletown, DE
01 June 2023

31366240R00182